国家重点中职示范校物流专业精品系列规划教材
广东省物流行业协会"工学结合"实践项目成果

——中职课堂任务引领教学改革教材

物流英语

主　编◎程大淼
副主编◎方金花
参　编◎王　丹
　　　　程嘉辉

华中科技大学出版社
http://www.hustp.com
中国·武汉

内 容 提 要

本书是中等职业学校物流专业的英语教材。本书的编写以中等职业学校对学生的培养方向为依据,注重培养学生的应用能力,取材联系实际、针对性强。本书有八个教学单元及附录,每个单元均包括课文、对话、单词、注解、知识积累、练习。其中,课文和对话的编排方式多样、图文并茂、简明易懂,附录中把物流常见的部分习惯用语列举出来,便于老师和学生查阅,同时也便于自学者查阅。所选内容题材涉及物流概念、包装、仓储、配送、国际物流、物流单证及物流信息技术。

本书可作为中等职业学校物流专业教学用书,同时也非常适合作为物流领域从业人员的培训教材。

图书在版编目(CIP)数据

物流英语/程大霖主编.—武汉:华中科技大学出版社,2013.3(2023.7重印)
ISBN 978-7-5609-7334-0

Ⅰ.①物… Ⅱ.①程… Ⅲ.①物流-英语-中等专业学校-教材 Ⅳ.①H31

中国版本图书馆 CIP 数据核字(2011)第 176199 号

物流英语 程大霖 主编

策划编辑:何 赟
责任编辑:何 赟
封面设计:潘 群
责任校对:何 欢
责任监印:徐 露

出版发行:华中科技大学出版社(中国•武汉) 电话:(027)81321913
　　　　　武汉市东湖新技术开发区华工科技园 邮编:430223
录　　排:华中科技大学惠友文印中心
印　　刷:广东虎彩云印刷有限公司
开　　本:787mm×1092mm　1/16
印　　张:8.25
字　　数:210 千字
版　　次:2023 年 7 月第 1 版第 15 次印刷
定　　价:22.00 元

本书若有印装质量问题,请向出版社营销中心调换
全国免费服务热线:400-6679-118　　竭诚为您服务
版权所有　侵权必究

国家重点中职示范校物流专业精品系列规划教材
广东省物流行业协会"工学结合"实践项目成果
编审委员会

顾　问	鲁修禄	副主任	广东省发展和改革委员会
	杨细平	副厅长	广东省交通运输厅
	刘文彬	处长	广东省发展和改革委员会
	黄建明	处长	广东省经济和信息化委员会
	余楚风	区长	广州市白云区政府
	丁　岩	副区长	广州市花都区政府
	谢　红	处长	广东省知识产权局
	张　燕	调研员	广东省经济和信息化委员会
	林殿盛	副处长	广州市交通委员会
	陈有文	主任	广东省物流标准化技术委员会
	陈功玉	主任	中山大学现代物流技术与管理研究中心
主　任	马仁洪	常务副会长、秘书长	广东省物流行业协会
副主任	梁玉霞	常务副秘书长	广东省物流行业协会
	许琳伟	主任	广东省职业技术教育学会物流专业指导委员会
	胡　梅	主任	广东省物流行业协会教育培训工作委员会
	胡学兰	副主任	广州市教育局教学研究室
特约编审	谢珍祥	副局长	广东省职业训练局
	邓庆宁	校长	广东省惠州商业学校
	杨柏弟	校长	佛山市南海区信息技术学校
	杨　敏	院长	广州市交通技师学院
	丘　文	校长	惠州工业科技学校
	胡　龙	校长	深圳市宝安职业技术学校
	杨志勇	校长	广州市商贸职业学校
	彭志斌	校长	佛山市顺德区陈村职业技术学校
	秦胜利	校长	广东省石油化工职业技术学校

张立波	校长	广州市财经职业技术学校
林　雄	校长	广东省海洋工程职业技术学校
周发茂	校长	广东省贸易职业技术学校
梁泽洪	校长	佛山市顺德区陈登职业技术学校
李国兴	校长	深圳市博伦职业技术学校
陈克虎	校长	东莞市常平镇黄水职业中学
邓　兵	校长	佛山市南海区盐步职业技术学校
邓　宁	校长	广东省财经职业技术学校
邓　联	校长	湛江财贸中等专业学校
石伟坤	校长	广东省东莞市威远职业高级中学
李驰稳	校长	江门市新会冈州职业技术学校
黄广旭	副校长	深圳市华强职业技术学校
袁吉玉	副校长	佛山市顺德区陈村职业技术学校
刘为民	副校长	广州市番禺区岭东职业技术学校
李文娟	校长	佛山市东立鳌云职业技术学校
林　荫	副校长	广东省汕头市澄海职业技术学校
刘龙山	院长	清远市技师学院
黄　志	院长	广东省技师学院
陈俊鸿	校长	广东省机械高级技工学校
阎子刚	校长	广东省交通运输高级技工学校
于锦杰	校长	湛江市高级技工学校
李志明	校长	广东省工业高级技工学校
胡利平	校长	江门市新会高级技工学校
崔险峰	校长	广东省电子信息技工学校
刘伟清	董事长	广东省航运集团有限公司
李志安	董事长	广东省惠州金泽集团
吴剑平	董事长	深圳市粤钢松山物流有限公司
陈拱龙	董事长	佛山市粤泰冷库物流投资有限公司
叶　斌	董事长	广州市易通四方网络科技有限公司
徐　龙	董事长	中国移动通信集团广东有限公司
夏　阳	董事长	广东三江实业发展有限公司
吴棋伟	董事长	广东天润物流市场发展有限公司
黄慧星	总经理	广东省华大物流总公司
林广宏	董事长	广州市宏峰物流有限公司
陈金平	董事长	深圳市金鹏物流园
刘发书	副总经理	广东省广新外贸集团有限公司
高艺林	总经理	广州市商业储运公司
李金平	董事长	广东林安物流发展有限公司
梁志成	总经理	中国外运广东有限公司
李凯乐	总经理	广东邮政物流配送服务有限公司
贾坎森	董事长	广州海心沙实业总公司
戴敏华	副总经理	广州市益达信息科技有限公司

梁耀权	副总经理	肇庆市致美物流有限公司
刘兴富	总经理	深圳市安必行物流顾问有限公司
王 宏	总经理	广州拜尔冷链聚胺酯科技有限公司
陈恒杰	总经理	广州市泰邦物流有限公司
张亚东	董事长	深圳宝鼎威物流有限公司
欧阳杰	总经理	广东东部物流有限公司
封建中	总经理	中山市秦粤物流有限公司
殷王龙	董事长	广州德镱数码技术有限公司
王熙祺	董事长	中外运瑞驰物流有限公司
张鸿飞	总经理	广州市盈致自动识别技术有限公司
郑泽民	董事长	广州天智市场开发有限公司
黄小燕	总经理	广州市亦立天然食品有限公司
蔡 军	物流总监	广州华新商贸有限公司
黄爱娟	总裁	广州城市之星运输有限公司
朱汉辉	执行董事	江门大昌慎昌食品加工仓储有限公司
张 艳	董事长	江门市安捷物流有限公司
李印铸	总裁	惠州港务集团有限公司
曾永青	所长	广州市食品工业研究所
田方人	董事长特助	顺德区北滘港货运联营有限公司
李素萍	总经理	广东东立商贸物流有限公司
何 望	总经理	广州保畅国际物流有限公司
徐明福	总经理	广州市高天文化机构
张晶林	总经理	广州市宏峰物流有限公司
冯展培	总经理	广州和笙富物流有限公司
时洪奎	总经理助理	广州市商业储运公司
卢慧华	总经理	广州青年书业有限公司
艾奇飞	总经理	烽火通信科技股份有限公司
陈 琳	总经理	广州巴斯特展览有限公司
谭衍诚	总经理	广州长盛永达贸易有限公司
梁慧莹	总编助理	《广东物流》杂志
姚 飞	总经理	广州壹加投资发展有限公司
谭锡棠	总经理	广州宏昌实业有限公司
曾会林	总经理	香港大光集团
吴桂标	总裁	柏亚国际集团有限公司

总序 > > >

  世界职业教育发展的经验和我国职业教育发展的历程都表明,职业教育是提高国家核心竞争力的要素。职业教育的这一重要作用,主要体现在两个方面。其一,职业教育承载着满足社会需求的重任,是培养为社会直接创造价值的高素质劳动者和专门人才的教育。职业教育既是经济发展的需要,又是促进就业的需要。其二,职业教育还承载着满足个性发展需求的重任,是促进青少年成才的教育。因此,职业教育既是保证教育公平的需要,又是教育协调发展的需要。

  这意味着,职业教育不仅有自己的特定目标——满足社会经济发展的人才需求,以及与之相关的就业需求,而且有自己的特殊规律——促进不同智力群体的个性发展,以及与之相关的智力开发。

  长期以来,由于我们对职业教育作为一种类型教育的规律缺乏深刻的认识,加之学校职业教育又占据绝对主体地位,因此职业教育与经济、与企业联系不紧,导致职业教育的办学未能冲破"供给驱动"的束缚;由于与职业实践结合不紧密,职业教育的教学也未能跳出学科体系的框架,所培养的职业人才,其职业技能的"专"、"深"不够,工作能力不强,与行业、企业的实际需求及我国经济发展的需要相距甚远。实际上,这也不利于个人通过职业这个载体实现自身所应有的职业生涯的发展。

  因此,要遵循职业教育的规律,强调校企合作、工学结合,"在做中学","在学中做",就必须进行教学改革。职业教育教学应遵循"行动导向"的教学原则,强调"为了行动而学习"、"通过行动来学习"和"行动就是学习"的教育理念,让学生在由实践情境构成的、以过程逻辑为中心的行动体系中获取过程性知识,去解决"怎么做"(经验)和"怎么做更好"(策略)的问题,而不是在由专业学科构成的、以架构逻辑为中心的学科体系中去追求陈述性知识,只解决"是什么"(事实、概念等)和"为什么"(原理、规律等)的问题。由此,作为教学改革核心的课程,就成为职业教育教学改革成功与否的关键。

  当前,在学习和借鉴国内外职业教育课程改革成功经验的基础上,工作过程导向的课程开发思想已逐渐为职业教育战线所认同。所谓工作过程,是"在企业里为完成一件工作任务并获得工作成果而进行的一个完整的工作程序",是一个综合的、时刻处于运动状态但结构相对固定的系统。与之相关的工作过程知识,是情境化的职业经验知识与普适化的系统科学知识的交集,它"不是关于单个事务和重复性质工作的知识,而是在企业内部关系中将不同的子工作予以连接的知识"。以工作过程逻辑展开的课程开发,其内容编排以典型的职业工作任务及实际的职业工作过程为参照系,按照完整行动所特有的"资讯、决策、计划、实施、检查、评价"结构,实现学科体系的解构与行动体系的重构,实现于变化的、具体的工作过程之中获取不变的思维过程和完整的工作训练,实现实体性技术、规范性技术通过过程性技术的物化。

近年来,教育部在中等职业教育领域组织了我国职业教育史上最大的职业教育师资培训项目——中德职教师资培训项目和国家级骨干师资培训项目。这些骨干教师通过学习、了解,接受先进的教学理念和教学模式,结合中国的国情,开发了更适合中国国情、更具有中国特色的职业教育课程模式。

华中科技大学出版社结合我国正在探索的职业教育课程改革,邀请我国职业教育领域的专家、企业技术专家和企业人力资源专家,特别是国家示范校、接受过中德职教师资培训或国家级骨干教师培训的中职院校的骨干教师,为支持、推动这一课程开发应用于教学实践,进行了有意义的探索——相关教材的编写。

华中科技大学出版社的这一探索,有两个特点。

第一,课程设置针对专业所对应的职业领域,邀请相关企业的技术骨干、人力资源管理者及行业著名专家和院校骨干教师,通过访谈、问卷和研讨,提出职业工作岗位对技能型人才在技能、知识和素质方面的要求,结合目前中国中职教育的现状,共同分析、讨论课程设置存在的问题,通过科学合理的调整、增删,确定课程门类及其教学内容。

第二,教学模式针对中职教育对象的特点,积极探讨提高教学质量的有效途径,根据工作过程导向课程开发的实践,引入能够激发学习兴趣、贴近职业实践的工作任务,将项目教学作为提高教学质量、培养学生能力的主要教学方法,把适度够用的理论知识按照工作过程来梳理、编排,以促进符合职业教育规律的、新的教学模式的建立。

在此基础上,华中科技大学出版社组织出版了这套规划教材。我始终欣喜地关注着这套教材的规划、组织和编写。华中科技大学出版社敢于探索、积极创新的精神,应该大力提倡。我很乐意将这套教材介绍给读者,衷心希望这套教材能在相关课程的教学中发挥积极作用,并得到读者的青睐。我也相信,这套教材在使用的过程中,通过教学实践的检验和实际问题的解决,不断得到改进、完善和提高。我希望,华中科技大学出版社能继续发扬探索、研究的作风,在建立具有中国特色的高等职业教育的课程体系的改革之中,做出更大的贡献。

是为序。

教育部职业技术教育中心研究所
学术委员会秘书长
《中国职业技术教育》杂志主编
中国职业技术教育学会理事、
教学工作委员会副主任、
职教课程理论与开发研究会主任
姜大源　教授
2011 年 6 月 6 日

前言

随着社会的发展和进步，人们享受着快捷、安全的生活，生活质量的提高得益于物流行业的发展，物流发展水平也正成为衡量一个国家综合国力、经济运行质量和社会组织管理效率的重要指标之一。在经济全球化的今天，现代物流在世界范围内已经成为具有发展潜力的新兴产业，所以掌握现代物流理念、先进的物流技术、国际化的运营模式，迅速改进管理水平，尽快与国际接轨，是中国物流企业不能回避的挑战。

我国企业要想迅速融入全球化并在其中得到高额回报，必须以高效率、高质量的金融流、信息流、人力流和物流系统作为支撑。但是目前全国掌握现代物流基本理念，擅长物流系统运作管理，物流操作技术熟练的人才十分匮乏。这就需要我们努力改变现状，为加快我国现代物流管理和技术人才的培养尽我们微薄之力。为使物流专业职业技术教育和物流企业职业培训符合现代物流发展的需要，满足一线物流人才实际技能培养和岗位培训的渴求，我们组织有丰富教学经验的教师深入物流企业一线进行实地了解、考察和观摩，为编写本教材获得第一手宝贵资料。本教材由一线英语教师和物流教师共同完成，吸纳了国内外最新物流实验和理论成果，采用了最新的物流理念与技术，顺应了职业技术教育的特点与需要，内容框架结构合理，简单易学，综合课程模块与职业资格取证挂钩(学与练相结合，加强实践、实训课程建设)，图文并茂，附录中提供了大量物流术语及解释和发音(是一本很好的工具书)，体现学生自主学习、探究学习、合作学习和教学方法、学习方法的改革。总的说来，这本教材既能适应职业培训的需要，又能满足自学者的需求。

在编写本书时，我们从社会实际需求出发，为了适应中等职业学校物流专业英语教学的需要，根据职业学校学生培养目标和要求，针对中职学生英语基础比较薄弱且水平参差不齐的现状，为了使学生学有所获、学有所得，本书体现了分层次教学的特点。在每一单元技能训练模块中，根据难易程度分成两个对话(交流篇)和两个基础知识短文(描述篇)，由浅入深，由简到繁，循序渐进，选材得当，设计多样，图文并茂，讲练结合，难度适宜。

本书由程大霖(广东省机械高级技工学校)任主编，方金花(广东省高级技工学校)，王丹(深圳市宝安职业技术学校)和 程嘉辉(广东省贸易职业技术学校)参编。

本书在编写过程中，参考了大量的书籍、文献等，作者已尽可能在参考文献中详细列出，在此对这些前辈、专家及学者深表谢意。引证材料可能有所疏漏,在此深表歉意。本书还得到了广东省机械高级技工学校刘碧云主任以及骆立文、王香老师和英语教研组全体教师的帮助和支持,在此谨表谢意。

编　者

2012 年 3 月于广州

目录 >>>

Unit One Introduction of Logistics	1
Text One Approaching Logistics(走进物流)	1
Dialogue One Campus Chatting(校园聊天)	3
Text Two Definition and Classification of Logistics(物流定义与分类)	4
Dialogue Two Visiting a Logistics Company(参观物流公司)	6
Unit Two Packaging	10
Text One What is Packaging?(包装是什么?)	10
Dialogue One What's Happened to Jane?(简发生了什么事?)	12
Text Two Functions of Packaging(包装的功能)	12
Dialogue Two Why Did the Article Get Damaged?(为什么商品会受损?)	14
Unit Three Warehousing	18
Text One Knowing Warehouse(了解仓库)	18
Dialogue One A Warehouse Keeper's Job(仓库管理员的工作)	20
Text Two An Introduction to Warehousing(介绍仓储)	21
Dialogue Two Understanding Inventory Management(了解库存管理)	23
Unit Four Distribution Center	28
Text One Knowing Distribution(了解配送)	28
Dialogue One What Are the Functions of Distribution Center?(配送中心的功能有哪些?)	30
Text Two Introduction of Distribution Center(配送中心介绍)	31
Dialogue Two A Distribution Agreement(销售协议)	32
Unit Five Transportation	37
Text One What is Transportation?(运输是什么?)	37
Dialogue One Let Apples Make More Money(让苹果挣更多的钱)	39
Text Two Functions of Transportation(运输功能)	39
Dialogue Two How Do Apples Make More Money?(苹果怎样挣更多的钱?)	41
Unit Six International Logistics	46
Text One Trends in International Logistics(国际物流未来趋势)	46

  Dialogue One Changing the Port of Unloading(改变卸货港) ………………… 48
  Text Two Global Intermediaries of International Logistics(国际物流的中介) ……… 50
  Dialogue Two Knowing about Containers(了解集装箱) …………………………… 51
Unit Seven Logistics Documents ……………………………………………………… 56
  Text One Introduction of Logistics Documents(物流单证的介绍) ………………… 56
  Dialogue One Knowing the Business Letters(了解商务信函) ……………………… 58
  Text Two Knowing Some Logistics Documents(了解一些物流单证) ……………… 59
  Dialogue Two Talking About Bill of Lading(谈论提单) …………………………… 61
Unit Eight Logistics Information …………………………………………………… 66
  Text One Information Technology(信息技术) ……………………………………… 66
  Dialogue One How Important Information Is!(信息多么重要!) ………………… 68
  Text Two Logistics Information Technology(物流信息技术) ……………………… 69
  Dialogue Two What Magical Scanners!(多么神奇的扫描仪呀!) ………………… 71
附录 A 物流专业词汇 ……………………………………………………………………… 76
附录 B 其他常见物流术语 ………………………………………………………………… 80
附录 C 物流业务中常见的英文省略语 …………………………………………………… 92
附录 D 国际物流贸易术语 ………………………………………………………………… 99
附录 E 部分物流外贸单据样本 …………………………………………………………… 100
附录 F 试卷 ………………………………………………………………………………… 106
附录 G 答案 ………………………………………………………………………………… 114
参考文献 ……………………………………………………………………………………… 120

Unit One
Introduction of Logistics

Part One　Learning Target (学习目标)

1. To master primary terms about logistics.
2. To understand the basic activities and functions of logistics and to master the definition and classification of logistics.
3. To develop communication skills in talking about logistics.

Part Two　Learning Contents (学习内容)

Text One

Approaching Logistics(走进物流)

The word "logistics" literally and narrowly means "movement of goods". But in fact, it covers much more. It involves several activities such as transportation, storage, loading and unloading, handling, packaging, distribution processing, distribution and information processing, etc. A simple explanation of logistics is: "Logistics is to deliver or store the right goods in the right place at the right time, in the right way efficiently and at the lowest cost."

Logistics contributes to economy by creating time value, location value and distribution processing value. Logistics is so important that no marketing or production can succeed without logistics support. For most companies, 10%—35% of gross sales are logistics cost which is called the third source of profit. The modern logistics plays an important role on the stage of global economy. In China, in the first 10 months of 2010, total social logistics has reached more than 100 trillion yuan. We believe China's logistics industry will soon enter a higher level development.

Words and Phrases（单词与短语）

logistics /ləuˈdʒistiks/	n. 物流，后勤学
approach /əˈprəutʃ/	v. 接近，靠近
literally /ˈlitərəli/	adv. 字面上地，照字义地
involve /inˈvɔlv/	v. 包含，牵涉
load /ləud/	v. 装载
unload /ˌʌnˈləud/	v. 卸下
package /ˈpækidʒ/	v. 为……包装
distribution /ˌdistriˈbjuːʃən/	n. 配送
deliver /diˈlivə/	v. 递送
contribute /kənˈtribjuːt/	v. 贡献
value /ˈvælju/	n. 价值
marketing /ˈmɑːkitiŋ/	n. 销售，市场营销
production /prəˈdʌkʃən/	n. 生产
succeed /səkˈsiːd/	v. 成功
trillion /ˈtriljən/	n. 万亿，兆
stage /steidʒ/	n. 舞台，阶段，行程
distribution processing value	流通加工价值
gross sales	总销售额
the third source of profit	第三利润源
global economy	全球经济
information processing	信息处理
play an important role	起重要作用

Notes（注释）

1. The word "logistics" literally and narrowly means "movement of goods". "物流"这个单词从字面上狭义地理解就是"货物的移动"。

2. Logistics is to deliver or store the right goods in the right place at the right time, in the right way efficiently and at the lowest cost. 物流就是花最小的成本，把正确的货物、在恰当的时间、以恰当的方式高效率地进行递送或保存到恰当的地方。

3. For most companies, 10%—35% of gross sales are logistics cost which is called the third source of profit. 对于大部分公司，总销售额的10%～35%都是被称为第三利润源的物流成本。

Dialogue One

Campus Chatting(校园聊天)

(*Wang Lin is a technical school student whose major is logistics. His friend is talking about his study.*)

Zhang: Wang Lin, why did you choose logistics as your major?

Wang: Well, my father runs a small third-party logistics firm. He needs me to help him with his business.

Zhang: I guess you are really interested in logistics.

Wang: Well, I think modern logistics is one of the most challenging and exciting fields! But logistics courses are not easy, you know!

Zhang: I agree. What subjects do you study at school?

Wang: We study Storage Management, Electronic Commerce, Purchasing Management, Distribution and Transportation, etc. My favorite subject is Logistics Practice.

Zhang: Wow, that sounds exciting!

Wang: Yeah! Logistics will bring me a nice future, I believe.

 Words and Phrases(单词与短语)

challenging /ˈtʃæləndʒɪŋ/	*adj.* 挑战性的,有吸引力的
storage /ˈstɔːrɪdʒ/	*n.* 仓储,储存
management /ˈmænɪdʒmənt/	*n.* 管理
purchasing /ˈpɜːtʃəsɪŋ/	*n.* 采购
transportation /ˌtrænspɔːˈteɪʃən/	*n.* 运输
electronic commerce /iˌlekˈtrɒnɪk ˈkɒmɜːs/	电子商务
third-party logistics	第三方物流
Logistics Practice	物流实训

Notes（注释）

1. My father runs a small third-party logistics firm. 我父亲经营一家小型的第三方物流公司。

2. I think modern logistics is one of the most challenging and exciting fields! 我认为现代物流是最富挑战性和最激动人心的工作领域之一。

Text Two

Definition and Classification of Logistics（物流定义与分类）

1. Definition of Logistics（物流定义）

There are different definitions of logistics. In China, "logistics" means the physical movement of goods from the supplier point to the receiver point. Based on practical need, logistics organically integrates various basic functional activities including transportation, storage, loading and unloading, handling, package, distribution and information management, etc.

2. Classification of Logistics（物流分类）

There are also various classifications of logistics. According to its functions in manufacturing enterprises, logistics can be classified as Supply Logistics, Production Logistics, Distribution Logistics, Returned Logistics and Waste Material Logistics.

3. Activities in Logistics System（物流系统活动）

A logistics system can be made up of different functional activities. They may include customer service, demand forecasting, packaging, warehousing, inventory management, transportation, procurement, material handing, information management, waste disposal and return goods handling (reverse distribution).

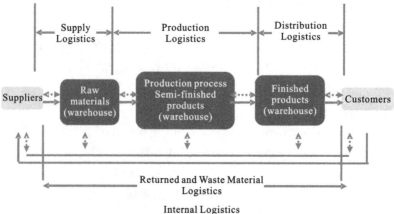

Words and Phrases（单词与短语）

definition /ˌdefiˈniʃən/	n. 定义,概念
classification /ˌklæsifiˈkeiʃən/	n. 分类
physical /ˈfizikəl/	adj. 物理的,物质的
integrate /ˈintigreit/	v. 整合
organically /ɔːˈgænikli/	adv. 有机地
various /ˈveəriəs/	adj. 各种各样的
basic /ˈbeisik/	adj. 基本的
functional /ˈfʌŋkʃənəl/	adj. 功能的,实用的
warehousing /ˈweəhauziŋ/	n. 仓储
inventory /ˈinvəntri/	n. 库存
procurement /prəˈkjuəmənt/	n. 采购
manufacturing enterprise	生产企业
Supply Logistics	供应物流
Production Logistics	生产物流
Distribution Logistics	分销物流
Returned Logistics	逆向物流
Waste Material Logistics	废弃物物流

Notes（注释）

1. In China, "logistics" means the physical movement of goods from the supplier point to the receiver point. Based on practical need, logistics organically integrates various basic functional activities including transportation, storage, loading and unloading, handling, package, distribution and information management, etc. 在中国,物流被定义为物品从供应地向接受地的实体流动过程,并根据实际需要,将运输、储存、装卸、搬运、包装、配送、信息处理等基本功能实现有机结合。

2. They may include customer service, demand forecasting, packaging, warehousing, inventory management, transportation, procurement, material handing, information management, waste disposal and return goods handling(reverse distribution). 物流功能活动可以包括客户服务、需求预测、包装、仓储、库存管理、运输、采购、物资搬运、信息管理、废物处理和退货处理(逆向物流)。

Dialogue Two

Visiting a Logistics Company (参观物流公司)

(*Mr. White, the customer, is visiting Linda's company.*)

Linda: Mr. White, let me show you around.

White: That's helpful! How large is your logistics park?

Linda: 8000 square meters. Here is our warehouse. Our company mainly engaged in third-party storage management and warehouse leasing.

White: It's much larger than I expected!

Linda: Look, we can see the highway from here.

White: Yeah! The traffic here is very convenient!

Linda: Wish you could cooperate with us. We can provide you a variety of goods inventory and we have special concessions on predominant goods or long-term contract.

White: I'm interested in it. Perhaps we'll have the cooperation soon.

Linda: It's good to hear that. We are looking forward to cooperating with you.

 Words and Phrases (单词与短语)

company /ˈkʌmpəni/	n. 公司
customer /ˈkʌstəmə/	n. 顾客
square /skweə/	adj. 平方的,正方的
warehouse /ˈweəhaus/	n. 仓库
engage /inˈgeidʒ/	v. 从事,参加
service /ˈsəːvis/	n. 服务
lease /liːs/	v. 租
traffic /ˈtræfik/	n. 交通
convenient /kənˈvinjənt/	adj. 方便的,便利的
cooperate /kəuˈɔpəreit/	v. 合作
contract /ˈkɔntrækt/	n. 合同
possibility /ˌpɔsəˈbiliti/	n. 可能性
concession /kənˈseʃn/	n. 优惠
predominant /priˈdɔminənt/	adj. 最显著的

 Notes (注释)

1. Our company mainly engaged in third-party storage management and warehouse

leasing. 我们公司主要从事第三方仓储管理和仓库租赁业务。

2. The traffic here is very convenient! 周围的交通是非常便利的!

3. We have special concessions on predominant goods or long-term contract. 对于大宗货物和租期较长的合同,我们都有特别的优惠。

Knowledge accumulation（知识积累）

1. Logistics is a hot topic in China. 中国掀起了物流热。

2. I wish to make logistics my lifetime career. 我愿把物流作为我的终身事业。

3. Logistics is the part of the supply chain process. 物流是供应链过程的组成部分。

4. Logistics is a unique global "pipeline". 物流是独特的全球通道。

5. Logistics is unique, and it never stops! 物流是独特的,它从不停止。

6. Logistics is concerned with getting products and services where they are needed and when they are desired. 物流所涉及的是在需要的时候和在需要的地方去获取产品和服务。

7. Logistics is related to the effective and efficient flow of materials and information. 物流所涉及的是物料和信息有效、快速的流动。

8. The overall goal of logistics is to achieve a targeted level of customer service at the lowest total cost. 物流的总目标是以最低的总成本实现客户服务的目标水平。

9. Logistics must be managed as a core competency. 物流必须作为一个核心竞争力来管理。

10. Logistics service is the balance between service priority and cost. 物流服务是服务优先与成本间的平衡。

Exercises（练习）

1. **Translate the following phrases/sentences into Chinese/English（英汉互译）.**

1) distribution processing value　＿＿＿＿＿＿＿＿＿＿＿＿＿＿＿＿

2) 生产物流　＿＿＿＿＿＿＿＿＿＿＿＿＿＿＿＿

3) loading and unloading　＿＿＿＿＿＿＿＿＿＿＿＿＿＿＿＿

4) 供应物流　＿＿＿＿＿＿＿＿＿＿＿＿＿＿＿＿

5) the third profit of source　＿＿＿＿＿＿＿＿＿＿＿＿＿＿＿＿

6) 信息处理　＿＿＿＿＿＿＿＿＿＿＿＿＿＿＿＿

7) 物流如此重要,如果离开物流,没有一次市场营销或生产会成功完成。

＿＿＿＿＿＿＿＿＿＿＿＿＿＿＿＿＿＿＿＿＿＿＿＿＿＿＿＿＿＿＿＿＿＿

8) I think modern logistics is one of the most challenging and exciting fields!

＿＿＿＿＿＿＿＿＿＿＿＿＿＿＿＿＿＿＿＿＿＿＿＿＿＿＿＿＿＿＿＿＿＿

9) Logistics is to deliver or store the right goods at the right place, at the right time, in the right way efficiently and at the lowest cost.

＿＿＿＿＿＿＿＿＿＿＿＿＿＿＿＿＿＿＿＿＿＿＿＿＿＿＿＿＿＿＿＿＿＿

10) 现代物流在世界经济的舞台上发挥着重要的作用。
_____

2. Answer the following questions in English(回答问题).

1) What is logistics according to Chinese stardard explanation?
_____

2) What is the classification of logistics?
_____

3) Does "logistics" simply mean "movement of the goods"?
_____

4) What do logistics activities include?
_____

3. Choose the best answers(选择题).

(　　)1) _____ is called the third source of profit.
   A. Packaging　　　　　　　　　B. Transportation
   C. both A and B　　　　　　　　D. Logistics

(　　)2) Which one is not a logistics activity?
   A. Packaging.　　　　　　　　　B. Transportation.
   C. Production.　　　　　　　　　D. Storage.

(　　)3) Which word is closely related to "movement of goods"?
   A. Marketing.　　　　　　　　　B. Transportation.
   C. Consumption.　　　　　　　　D. Production.

(　　)4) What does Returned Logistics mean?
   A. 绿色物流　　B. 回收物流　　C. 废弃物物流　　D. 供应物流

(　　)5) What does Supply Logistics mean?
   A. 绿色物流　　B. 回收物流　　C. 废弃物物流　　D. 供应物流

(　　)6) The word "logistics" _____ means "movement of goods"?
   A. simply　　　　　　　　　　　B. literally
   C. narrowly　　　　　　　　　　D. both B and C

(　　)7) _____ means to deliver goods between the supplier point and the receiver point.
   A. Marketing　　B. Transportation　　C. Packaging　　D. Repairing

(　　)8) In logistics, _____ is another kind of flow different from material flow.
   A. information flow　　　　　　B. capital flow
   C. people flow　　　　　　　　 D. product flow

(　　)9) What is logistics?
   A. Material movement.　　　　　B. Purchasing goods.
   C. Producing goods.　　　　　　D. None of above.

(　　)10) Which one is correct?
   A. Logistics is important.

B. Logistics should be ignored(忽视).

C. Logistics means transportation.

D. Logistics means shipping.

4. **Reading passage(阅读小短文).**

Third-party logistics (3PL) is the way of outsourcing. It involves using external parts to perform some of the logistics activities. If, for example, a company which has its own warehousing facilities decides to employ external transportation, this would be an example of third-party logistics. Why does the company need 3PL? There are at least three reasons: saving time, sharing responsibility, and someone else do it better.

根据短文内容选择最合适的答案。

( )1) 3PL means _____.

    A. third-party logistics   B. a party

    C. three parts   D. logistics

( )2) "Outsourcing" means _____.

    A. 出国   B. 输出   C. 外包   D. 采购

( )3) Which is wrong?

    A. 3PL is useless.   B. 3PL is a type of logistics.

    C. 3PL is helpful.   D. 3PL can do better sometimes.

Unit Two
Packaging

Part One　Learning Target (学习目标)

1. To master primary terms about packaging.
2. To master basic knowledge about packaging.
3. To develop communication skills in talking about packaging.

Part Two　Learning Contents (学习内容)

Text One

What is Packaging? (包装是什么?)

1. The Definition of Packaging(包装的概念)

In short, packaging is "a means of ensuring safe delivery of a product to the consumer in good condition and at lowest cost". There are two forms of packaging: the industrial packaging and the consumer packaging.

2. The Importance of Packaging(包装的重要性)

Every buyer expects that his goods will reach him in perfect condition. To a buyer nothing is more infuriating than to find his goods damaged or part missing on arrival. It has been estimated that as much as 70% of all cargos loss could be prevented by proper packaging and marking.

1) Packaging may affect production, as production employees often need to package the goods. The size, shape, and material of the package greatly affect the labor efficiency.

2) Although packaging is not as costly as transportation, it still makes up of integrated logistics cost. Furthermore, most goods require protection while moving through the integrated logistics system.

3) Packaging can help to prevent theft and avoid damage and also help to promote the sales and inform the customer.

Words and Phrases（单词与短语）

infuriate /in'fjuərieit/	v. 激怒
buyer /'baiə/	n. 消费者，买方
estimate /'estimeit/	v. 估量，评价
cargo /'kɑːgəu/	n. 货物
loss /lɔs/	n. 损失，亏损
trade /treid/	n. 贸易，交易
decision /di'siʒən/	n. 决策，决定
marking /'mɑːkiŋ/	n. 标记，标志
employee /im'plɔiiː/	n. 员工，雇员
efficiency /i'fiʃənsi/	n. 效率
material /mə'tiriəl/	n. 材料，原料
theft /θeft/	n. 偷窃，盗窃
delivery /di'livəri/	n. 送交，传递
perfect condition	完好无损
logistics decisions	物流决策
integrated logistics	一体化物流，综合物流
consumer packaging	销售包装
attribute to	把某事归因与某人、某事

Notes（注释）

1. Nothing is more infuriating to a buyer than to find his goods damaged or part missing on arrival. 对于买方来说，没有比发现自己所购买的商品被损坏或者部分缺失更令人恼火的。

2. Packaging may affect production, as production employees often need to package the goods. 包装或许影响生产，因为生产工人需要经常对产品进行包装处理。

Dialogue One

What's Happened to Jane? (简发生了什么事?)

(*Jane has just received a toy model which she has been waiting for a long time, but she is unhappy.*)

Tom: You look so upset. What's happened to you?

Jane: My toy model has arrived, but....

Tom: What?

Jane: The toy is damaged, and the most terrible thing is that some accessories are missing.

Tom: I'm sorry to hear that. I don't think either the packaging is right, or the packing box is strong enough. Maybe it was damaged during handling, storing or transportation. I think you should make a complaint to the seller.

Jane: Thanks a lot. I'll do it.

 Words and Phrases (单词与短语)

article /ˈɑːtɪkl/   n. 商品,物品
accessory /əkˈsesəri/   n. 配件,附件
seller /ˈselə/   n. 销售方,卖方
toy model   玩具模型

 Notes (注释)

The toy is damaged, and the most terrible thing is that some accessories are missing. 商品被损坏了,更让人气愤的是某些配件居然还丢失了。

Functions of Packaging(包装的功能)

1. Functions of Industrial Packaging(工业包装的功能)

Industrial packaging fulfils these functions:

1) To protect product from contamination which results from contacting with other goods, water damage, temperature changes, pilferage, and shocks in handling and transport.

In some cases, packages must be strong enough to support the products stacked on it.

2) To maximize ease handling in conjunction with materials handling and transportation. So it can improve the logistics efficiency.

3) To provide information about handling and identification.

2. Functions of Consumer Packaging（销售包装的功能）

Consumer packaging also refers to the interior package, or marketing package because the customer can see the package when the product is on the shelf. So the consumer packaging assists in marketing, promoting the product, advertising and giving information to customers.

 Words and Phrases（单词与短语）

contamination /kənˌtæməˈneiʃən/	n. 污染，弄脏
pilferage /ˈpilfərəridʒ/	n. 盗窃
shock /ʃɔk/	n. 冲击，震动
stack /stæk/	v. 堆积，堆垛
conjunction /kənˈdʒʌŋkʃən/	n. 结合，联合
maximize /ˈmæksəˌmaiz/	v. 使（某事物）增至最大限度
promote /prəˈməut/	v. 促进；推动；增进
identification /aiˌdentifiˈkeiʃən/	n. 识别，鉴定，身份证明
interior /inˈtiəriə/	adj. 内部的
advertising /ˈædvəˌtaiziŋ/	n. 广告，广告宣传
result from	产生于……，由……引起

 Notes（注释）

In some cases, packages must be strong enough to support the products stacked on it. 在某些情况下，货物的包装还需要承受堆放在其上方货物的重量。

Dialogue Two

Why Did the Article Get Damaged?（为什么商品会受损？）

Tom: I think the packaging is relevant.

Jane: I can't agree with you anymore.

Tom: The main problem lies in industrial packaging of the article.

Jane: What is industrial packaging?

Tom: Industrial packaging is also known as exterior packaging. The package is discarded before the products are placed on the shelf, so customers may never see this package. It is a method to protect the article from damage in transportation and handling.

Jane: Then that is to say industrial packaging is quite important and necessary to protect the goods from damage, isn't it?

Tom: Quite right. The packaging must be strong enough to withstand rough handling. Remember: Unprepared fight is horrible. Making preparations beforehand is important.

 Words and Phrases（单词与短语）

relevant /ˈreləvənt/	adj. 有关的,切题的
anymore /ˌeniˈmɔː/	adv. 目前,现在,不再
packaging /ˈpækidʒiŋ/	n. 包装,包装材料
fundamental /ˌfʌndəˈmentl/	adj. 基础的,根本的
method /ˈmeθəd/	n. 方法,手段
protect /prəˈtekt/	v. 保护,防护
transportation /ˌtrænspɔːˈteiʃən/	n. 运输
handling /ˈhændliŋ/	n. 搬运
industrial packaging	工业包装
that is to say	就是说,更确切地说
withstand rough handling	承受粗鲁的搬运

 Notes（注释）

1. The main problem lies in industrial packaging of the article. 主要问题就是货物的工业包装。

2. It is a method to protect the article from damage in transportation and handling. 它是一种能保护商品,以使商品在运输和搬运过程中免受损坏的方法。

3. Unprepared fight is horrible. Making preparations beforehand is important. 打无准备

之仗是可怕的。提前做准备是重要的。

Knowledge accumulation（知识积累）

1. Packaging widely used today has become a major point in the market competition of products. 今天,广泛使用的包装已成为产品市场竞争的主要竞争点。

2. Packaging is extremely important to warehousing and materials handling; people increasingly pay attention to it all over the world. 包装对仓储和物资搬运作业至关重要,它在全球日益受到关注。

3. Thanks to packaging, it makes products available anytime anywhere, that gives the consumers a lot of choice. 由于包装的存在,使得产品能在任何时候和任何地方都可得到,这给消费者极大的选择自由。

Exercises（练习）

1. Translate the following phrases/sentences into Chinese/English（英汉互译）.

1) industrial packaging　　_____
2) 一体化物流　　_____
3) consumer packaging　　_____
4) 物流决策　　_____
5) service level　　_____
6) 包装材料　　_____
7) Packaging is "a means of ensuring safe delivery of a product to the consumer in good condition and at lowest cost".

_____

8) 包装共有两种形式:工业包装与销售包装。

_____

9) The size, shape, and material of a package greatly affect labor efficiency.

_____

10) 销售包装有助于市场营销活动、产品促销、广告宣传以及向消费者传达信息。

_____

2. Answer the following questions in English（回答问题）.

1) What is packaging?

_____

2) What could make a buyer most upset?

_____

3) In the past, what was the role of packaging in trading field?

_____

4) Why does packaging affect production?
_____

3. Choose the best answers according to description(选择题).

( ) 1) How to prevent the cargo from damage and loss?
    A. Packaging.　　　　　　　　　　B. Parking.
    C. Both A and B　　　　　　　　　D. Handling.

( ) 2) Could all the cargos reach a buyer in perfect condition?
    A. Yes.　　　　　　　　　　　　　B. No.
    C. Not mentioned.　　　　　　　　D. Obscure.

( ) 3) Which activity would not be affected by packaging?
    A. Marketing.　　　　　　　　　　B. Transportation.
    C. Consumption.　　　　　　　　　D. Repairing.

( ) 4) How did logistician regard packaging in the past?
    A. Disregard.　　　　　　　　　　B. Neglect.
    C. Both A and B.　　　　　　　　　D. Consider.

( ) 5) How many percentages of integrated logistics costs come from packaging?
    A. Thirty.　　B. Seventy.　　C. Ten.　　D. Twenty.

( ) 6) Which factor of packaging would greatly affect labor efficiency?
    A. Size.　　　　　　　　　　　　　B. Shape.
    C. Material.　　　　　　　　　　　D. All of the previous options.

( ) 7) Which factor would affect the goods in handling and transportation?
    A. Pollution.　　　　　　　　　　B. Theft.
    C. Shock.　　　　　　　　　　　　D. All of the previous options.

( ) 8) Are goods put together with other ones always safe?
    A. Yes.　　　　　　　　　　　　　B. No.
    C. Not mentioned.　　　　　　　　D. Obscure.

( ) 9) What does identification information include?
    A. Place of origin.　　　　　　　　B. Brand.
    C. The name of article.　　　　　　D. Specification.

( ) 10) Handling information can not _____.
    A. protect goods　　　　　　　　　B. protect workers
    C. make handling more efficient　　D. make goods lighter

4. Reading passage(阅读小短文).

包装材料的介绍

Package materials consist of paper, plastic, wood, metal and glass. Paper is taking the biggest percentage(比例) among all packing materials. It can be used to make outer package, carton (paper box) and corrugated(起褶皱的) box. Paper is cheap, easy to shape and it is ventilated(通风的). Plastic is a new fast developed material, which is at low cost, strong, has good resistance(抵抗力) to water, acid(酸) and so on. Because of environmental protection wood has become the least proportion(部分) of the packing materials. It is used to make the wood box. Metal, exactly aluminum（铝）is to make cans for drinks, like Coca Cola, which is easy to recycle. Glass is mainly used to fill the liquid, like chemical products and liquors(酒).

根据短文内容选择问题最合适的答语。

( )1) Tom: Which is taking the biggest percentage of the packing materials?
  Jane: _____.
  A. Plastic   B. Wood   C. Paper   D. Glass

( )2) Tom: Which kind of package material has become the least proportion because of environmental protection?
  Jane: _____.
  A. Plastic   B. Wood   C. Paper   D. Glass

( )3) Tom: Can aluminum be made into cans for drinks?
  Jane: _____.
  A. No   B. Uncertainty   C. Yes   D. Sorry

Unit Three
Warehousing

Part One Learning Target (学习目标)

1. To understand the role of warehousing.
2. To know the activities of warehousing.
3. To learn the functions of warehousing.
4. To develop communication skill in introducing the warehouse.
5. To grasp writing skill in introducing the warehouse.

Part Two Learning Contents (学习内容)

Text One

Knowing Warehouse (了解仓库)

1. Warehouse (仓库)

A warehouse (or store) may be defined as a facility which can provide efficient handling and storage of goods and materials in a planned space. There are estimated 750000 warehouse facilities worldwide, including professionally managed warehouses, as well as company stockrooms, garages, self-store facilities, and even garden sheds.

2. Types of Warehouses (仓库的类型)

Warehouses are usually divided into private warehouses, public warehouses and contract warehouse. While according to the storage purpose, warehouses are divided into deliver-center warehouses, storage-center warehouses and logistics-center warehouses.

The private warehouses are owned by the firms using them. So the firms themselves have authority to make decision over all activities in the warehouses.

Public warehouses offer more flexibility for the users since there is no capital investment on the equipments.

Contract warehousing is a long term, mutually beneficial arrangement which provides special warehousing and logistics services for the customer.

Words and Phrases（单词与短语）

private /ˈpraivit/	adj. 私有的
contract /ˈkɔntrækt/	n. 合同
equipment /iˈkwipmənt/	n. 设备
capital investment	资金投资
deliver-center warehouse	配送中心型仓库
storage-center warehouse	存储中心型仓库
logistics-center warehouse	物流中心型仓库
mutually beneficial	互惠

Notes（注释）

1. A warehouse (or store) may be defined as a facility which can provide efficient handling and storage of goods and materials in a planned space. 仓库(货库)可以定义为在计划空间环境里为商品和物料提供有效的处理及仓储的设施。

2. There are estimated 750000 warehouse facilities worldwide, including professionally managed warehouses, as well as company stockrooms, garages, self-store facilities, and even garden sheds. 全世界估计有75万个仓库设施，包括专业管理仓库、公司仓库、车库、私人仓库、甚至花园小屋。

3. Private warehouses are owned by the firms using them. So the firms themselves have authority to make decision over all activities in the warehouses. 私有仓库是由使用它们的公司自有。因此企业本身对仓库所有活动有权自主决定。

4. Public warehouses offer more flexibility for the users since there is no capital investment on the equipments. 由于不需要对设备进行投资，因此使用公共仓库有更大的灵活性。

5. Contract warehousing is a long term, mutually beneficial arrangement which provides special warehousing and logistics services for the customer. 合同仓储是一个长期的双方互惠协定，(仓储设施的经营人)为其客户提供专门的仓储和物流服务。

Dialogue One

A Warehouse Keeper's Job(仓库管理员的工作)

(*Zhang Gang is a warehouse keeper of P&G. Wu Hua is a student majoring in logistics.*)

Zhang: How do you do? Welcome to our warehouse. Let me introduce myself first. I am a warehouse keeper and I am responsible for the management of goods.

Wu: Nice to meet you. Wow! What a modern warehouse! Excuse me, what procedures will you carry out after the goods arrive at the warehouse?

Zhang: First indoor operation, second warehouse management, finally warehouse operation.

Wu: What is the indoor operation?

Zhang: It includes arranging storehouses, checking the goods, enrolling the goods accurately, loading and laying them up in standard.

Wu: And the warehouse management?

Zhang: Checking the products and equipment often, keeping the warehouse clean and safe, standardizing each operation and gathering the information accurately and timely.

Wu: How about the warehouse operation?

Zhang: When the goods are out of the warehouse, we must carry out the following warehouse procedures: checking the quantity of the goods, loading the goods and laying them up in standard, providing the goods according to the shipment list, saving and filing the bills of document.

Wu: Now I know how important a warehouse keeper is. Thank you very much!

Zhang: You are welcome.

 Words and Phrases (单词与短语)

major /ˈmeidʒə/	n. 专业　v. 主修
warehouse /ˈweəhaus/	n. 仓库
procedure /prəˈsiːdʒə/	n. 程序, 手续
indoor /ˈindɔː/	adj. 入库的

arrange /əˈreɪndʒ/	v. 安排
enroll /ɪnˈrəʊl/	v. 登记
equipment /ɪˈkwɪpmənt/	n. 设备
regularly /ˈreɡjələli/	adv. 经常性地
standardize /ˈstændəˌdaɪz/	v. 使标准化
gather /ˈɡæðə/	v. 收集
responsible /rɪˈspɒnsəbl/	adj. 有责任的，负责任的
lay up	放置，储存
indoor operation	入库作业
warehouse management	仓库管理
warehouse operation	仓库操作

Notes（注释）

1. It includes arranging storehouses, checking the goods, enrolling the goods accurately, loading and laying them up in standard. 这有一系列程序，包括：安排仓位，核对物品，准确登记，规范装卸。

2. Checking the products and equipment often, keeping the warehouse clean and safe, standardizing each operation and gathering the information accurately and timely. 经常检查产品、设备，保持仓库清洁、安全，规范各项运作，信息汇总准确、及时。

3. When the goods are out of the warehouse, we must carry out the following warehouse procedures: checking the quantity of the goods, loading the goods and laying them up in standard, providing the goods according to the shipment list, saving and filing the bills of document. 货物出库时，必须履行以下仓库程序：核对出库货物数量，规范装卸，按出货单先后发放货物，出库单据保存归档。

An Introduction to Warehousing（介绍仓储）

1. Warehousing Activities（仓储活动）

Warehousing activity is an important link between the producer and the customer. Warehousing activities include receiving, transfer, storage, picking, and shipping.

2. Main Components of Warehousing（仓储的主要组成）

The three basic components of warehousing are warehouse, equipments, and people. Warehouse equipments include materials carrying equipments, storage racks and conveyor equipments.

3. The Role of Warehousing（仓储的作用）

Warehousing plays a key role in logistics and in building and keeping good relationship between supply chain partners.

Warehousing affects customer service level, sales and marketing success. Warehousing can link the production place and the consumer, or supplier and production place. Warehousing supports production by uniting internal materials and distributing raw materials to the production place at the right time. Warehousing also helps marketing to serve existing customers and develope new markets.

Words and Phrases（单词与短语）

receiving /riˈsiːviŋ/	n. 接收
transfer /trænsˈfəː/	n. 传送
storage /ˈstɔːridʒ/	n. 储存
picking /ˈpikiŋ/	n. 分拣
shipping /ˈʃipiŋ/	n. 装运
consumer /kənˈsjuːmə/	n. 消费者
internal /inˈtəːnl/	adj. 内部的
distribute /diˈstribjuːt/	v. 分配
existing /igˈzistiŋ/	adj. 目前的
increase /inˈkriːs/	v. 增加
materials carrying	物料搬运
storage rack	储存货架
conveyor equipment	传送设备
supply chain	供应链

Notes（注释）

1. Warehouse equipments include materials carrying equipments, storage racks and conveyor equipments. 仓储设备包括物料搬运设备、储存货架和传送设备。

2. Warehousing supports production by uniting internal materials and distributing raw materials to the production place at the right time. 仓储通过整合内部资源支持生产并在恰当的时间将原材料配送到生产点。

Dialogue Two

Understanding Inventory Management（了解库存管理）

(*Li Hai is a storekeeper of Dalian Shipping Company. Wu Gang is a clerk of a logistics company.*)

Li: Nice to meet you.

Wu: I'm glad to see you, too. Today I come here to learn how to manage the inventory.

Li: Oh, no problem. First allow me to show you around our warehouse. It is known that inventory is a large and costly investment. Better management of firm inventories can improve cash flow and return on investment.

Wu: You are right. What is your inventory goal?

Li: It is to achieve the desired customer service with the minimum inventory and lowest total cost.

Wu: What is the goal of your inventory management?

Li: It is to minimize inventory investment while still meeting the functional requirements.

Wu: And what is your inventory decision?

Li: Our inventory decision involves knowing how much to order and when to order.

Wu: Oh, I see. Thanks for your introduction in detail. If I have any chance, I will cooperate with you.

Li: You're welcome.

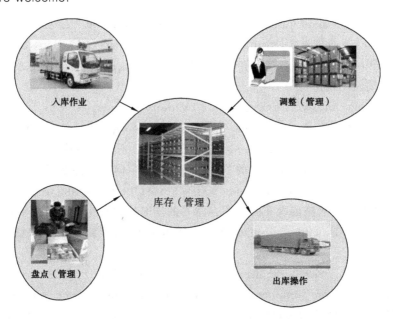

Words and Phrases（单词与短语）

inventory /ˈinvəntri/	n. 库存
firm /fə:m/	n. 公司
achieve /əˈtʃi:v/	v. 达到，实现
desire /diˈzaiə/	v. 渴望，希望
minimum /ˈminiməm/	adj. 最小的，最低的
minimize	把……减至最低数量
costly investment	高投资
functional requirements	功能需求
inventory decision	库存决策

Notes（注释）

1. Better management of firm inventories can improve cash flow and return on investment. 对库存的良好管理能够加快现金流动及提高投资回报。

2. It is to achieve the desired customer service with the minimum inventory and lowest total cost. 目标是以最低成本的库存达到满意的客户服务水平。

3. Our inventory decision involves knowing how much to order and when to order. 库存决策包括下订单的数量和时间两方面。

Knowledge accumulation（知识积累）

1. There are five main purposes of inventory within the firm: acting as a buffer, achieving economies of scale, balancing supply and demand, specialization, offering protection against uncertainties. 公司内部库存有五个主要作用：起到缓冲作用，实现规模经济，均衡供给和需求，专业化，防止不确定性。

2. If you keep an overstock of the inventory, expenses will incur not only in warehousing, but also in many other aspects, such as the capital cost and interest accruing to it, taxes, insurance and obsolescence cost. 如果过量库存，不仅会造成仓储费用而且在很多方面会产生费用，如资产成本和它所产生的利息，以及税收、保险和商品变成陈旧物的成本。

3. Just-in-time strategy ensures materials available for production while minimizing inventory. 及时盘存调节战略确保在降低库存水平的同时能得到生产所需的物料。

4. The goal of just-in-time purchasing is zero inventory. 及时盘存调节采购的目标是零库存。

5. Setting inventory levels requires downstream information from customers on demand, upstream information from suppliers on availability and information on current inventory levels. 制定库存水平需要下游客户需求信息、上游供应链可供信息和当前的库存水平信息。

6. Warehousing is not a new business, but it has gained new functions in modern logistics. 仓储不是新的行业,但它在现代物流中有了新的功能。

7. Inventory control can effectively reduce logistics cost. 库存控制能有效地降低物流成本。

8. Before deciding how much to order, the company needs to balance order-processing costs against inventory-carrying costs. 在决定下订单前,公司需要平衡订单处理成本和库存持有成本。

9. When the stock is near safety stock level, the material has to be reordered. 当库存接近安全库存时,材料必须重新订购。

Exercises（练习）

1. Translate the following phrases/sentences into Chinese/English（英汉互译）.

1) storage rack　　　　　　　　　　_____
2) private warehouse　　　　　　　 _____
3) indoor operation　　　　　　　　_____
4) 配送中心型仓库　　　　　　　　 _____
5) 资金回笼　　　　　　　　　　　 _____
6) 库存管理　　　　　　　　　　　 _____
7) I want to be a warehouse keeper in the future.
_____

8) People are the most important part of warehousing.
_____

9) 我想和老师一起参观一个仓库。
_____

10) 仓储对于一个公司很重要。
_____

2. Answer the following questions in English（回答问题）.

1) What does Zhang Gang do in Dialogue One?
_____

2) How does Wu Hua like Zhang Gang's warehouse?
_____

3) Is inventory management important for a firm?
_____

4) How many types are warehouses usually divided into?
_____

3. Choose the best answers according to description(选择题).

(　　)1) Li: Welcome to our warehouse.

Wang: _____
A. Yes. B. Thank you.
C. You are right. D. OK.

( ) 2) Hu: Is inventory management important for a firm?
Wu: _____
A. It is. B. No. C. I think so. D. Yes.

( ) 3) Li: What are the components of warehousing?
Wang: They are warehouse, _____ and people.
A. racks B. materials C. equipment D. firms

( ) 4) Hi! Let's _____ a warehouse together.
A. go B. visit C. come D. look

( ) 5) Gong: Thank you for introduction.
Ji: _____
A. It's my pleasure. B. No, thanks.
C. Never mind. D. Yes.

( ) 6) Wu: _____ is your warehousing business?
Li: Good.
A. Where B. How C. × D. Which

( ) 7) _____ isn't one of the warehousing activities in logistics system.
A. Shipping B. Picking
C. Storage D. Transportation

( ) 8) The warehouse is divided into private and _____ warehouse and contract warehousing.
A. public B. small C. large D. modern

( ) 9) An: Will you work carefully if you were a warehouse keeper?
Kang: _____
A. Of course. B. I will do that.
C. I will. D. No, I will.

( ) 10) Huang: If you are a manager, do you like public warehouse or private warehouse?
Cheng: _____
A. No. B. Yes.
C. I like public warehouse. D. Yes, I don't think so.

4. **Reading passage(阅读小短文).**

Li Haohao has just been employed(被雇用) by a forwarding(代理的) company at an airport. His job is to allocate(分配) the products to different shelves. With the help of the warehouse manager, he is getting himself acquainted(了解) with the work. One day, a truck stops at the gate. Li Haohao goes over and finds that a container chassis(底架) is at the gate and workers are discharging(卸) some electronic components(电子零件) in large cases. These cargos are to be exported to Korea and Singapore, they will be leaving this afternoon. So Li Haohao arranges two shelves near the other end of warehouse for these cargos. That way they can be shipped easier later. He is a clever man who can quickly learn how to work well.

根据短文内容选择问题最合适的答语。

(　　)1) Tom: Where has Li Haohao just been employed?

　　　　Jane: _____.

　　　　A. At an airport　　　　　　　　B. At a discharging company

　　　　C. At a forwarding company　　　D. At a logistics company

(　　)2) Tom: Is Li Haohao hardworking?

　　　　Jane: _____.

　　　　A. No　　　　　　　　　　　　B. Yes

　　　　C. Sorry, I don't know　　　　　D. No mentioned

(　　)3) Tom: What is his job?

　　　　Jane: He _____.

　　　　A. is a logistics manager

　　　　B. is a logistics agent

　　　　C. handles components

　　　　D. allocates the products to different shelves

Unit Four
Distribution Center

Part One Learning Target (学习目标)

1. To know the types of distribution and distribution center.
2. To understand the definition and functions of distribution and distribution center.
3. To develop communication skill in talking about distribution.

Part Two Learning Contents (学习内容)

Text One

Knowing Distribution (了解配送)

1. What is Distribution? (什么是配送?)

Distribution refers to dispatching the goods in the specific transportation mode.

In the rational economic area, according to the requirement of the customers, distribution is the operations for the items, which includes picking, processing, packaging, dividing and so on, and logistics activities of delivering the goods to designated place on time.

2. Types of Distribution (配送类型)

Distribution is classified into three types according to different organizers: delivery of distribution center, warehouse distribution and store distribution.

3. Operation Flow of Distribution (配送的运作流程)

There are nine steps in the operation flow of distribution: stock, loading, unloading and carrying, putting in storage, order picking, replenishing, order processing, distribution processing, distributing and delivering.

4. The Service Ways of Distribution (配送服务方式)

Distribution is a logistics link which contacts with the customers directly. To meet the need of users and consumers, there are different ways of distribution: timing distribution, distribution on time, express distribution, ration, timing and ration, timing and route and timely distribution.

Words and Phrases（单词与短语）

stock /stɔk/	v. 储备
replenishment /rɪˈplenɪʃmənt/	n. 补货
ration /ˈræʃən/	n. 定量
loading, unloading and carrying	装卸搬运
delivery of distribution center	配送中心配送
warehouse distribution	仓库配送
store distribution	商店配送
order processing	订单处理
distribution processing	流通加工
timing distribution	定时配送
distribution on time	准时配送
express distribution	快递配送
timing and ration	定时定量
timing and route	定时定路线
timely distribution	即时配送

Notes（注释）

1. Distribution refers to dispatching the goods in the specific transportation mode. 配送指的就是将货物按指定的运输方式发送货物。

2. In the rational economic area, according to the requirement of the customers, distribution is the operations for the items, which includes picking, processing, packaging, dividing and so on, and logistics activities of delivering the goods to designated place on time. 在经济合理区域内,根据客户的要求,配送就是对物品进行拣选、加工、包装、分割等作业,并按时送达指定地点的物流活动。

Dialogue One

What Are the Functions of Distribution Center? (配送中心的功能有哪些?)

(*Li Hai is a manager in Dalian Distribution Center. Wang Gang is a student from No. 2 Vocational School.*)

Wang: Nice to meet you, Mr. Li.

Li: Nice to meet you, too. Welcome. Can I help you?

Wang: I come here to learn something about your distribution center. Will you please introduce its functions?

Li: Oh! First, you should know it is different from the warehouse.

Wang: What are the differences? I can't wait to know them.

Li: Take it easy. I will tell you some functions about our distribution center. The distribution center is built for the moving of goods. It is located close to a major market. It performs many value-added activities. It handles most products in receiving, picking, packaging and shipping. It collects data in real time. It holds high-demand goods. It focuses on maximizing the profit while fulfilling customer delivery need.

Wang: It's very kind of you to tell me in detail. Thanks a lot.

Li: It's my pleasure.

Words and Phrases (单词与短语)

distribution /ˌdistriˈbjuːʃən/ n. 配给
locate /ləuˈkeit/ v. 坐落
perform /pəˈfɔːm/ v. 执行,履行
demand /diˈmaːnd/ n. 需求
maximize /ˈmæksəˌmaiz/ v. 最大化
profit /ˈprɔfit/ n. 收益,利润
fulfill /fulˈfil/ v. 实现,履行
focus on 焦点,重点,对……给予关注

Notes（注释）

1. It focuses on maximizing the profit while fulfilling customer delivery need. 配送中心在使利润最大化的同时履行客户送货需求。

2. It collects data in real time. 配送中心收集实时数据。

Introduction of Distribution Center（配送中心介绍）

1. What is the Distribution Center?（什么是配送中心？）

Distribution center is a logistics link. Its main function is to carry out physical distribution. In detail, it is a large and automated center designated to receive goods from various plants and suppliers, take orders, fill orders efficiently, and deliver goods to customers on time.

2. Operation Flow of Distribution Center（配送中心的运作流程）

There are seven steps in the operation flow of distribution center.

They are goods consolidating, storage, order picking, replenishing, order processing, sorting and distribution.

3. Types of Distribution Center（配送中心的类型）

1) Supply distribution center

2) Market distribution center

3) Storage distribution center

4. Functions Areas of the Distribution Center（配送中心的功能区）

The installation was designed to integrate the flow of product through the following functions areas of the distribution center: receiving area, value-added service (VAS) preparation area, VAS processing area, waste processing area, storage area and dispatching area.

5. Equipment of the Distribution Center（配送中心的设备）

The equipments include accumulation conveyors, belt inclines and declines, live rollers, sorters and diverts, waste processing conveyors and more.

live rollers　　belt inclines and declines　　accumulation conveyors　　sorters and diverts

Words and Phrases（单词与短语）

supply distribution center	供应型配送中心
market distribution center	销售型配送中心
storage distribution center	储存型配送中心
value-added service(VAS) preparation area	增值服务准备区
VAS processing area	增值服务加工区
waste processing area	废料处理区
storage area	储存区
dispatching area	发货区
accumulation conveyor	堆垛机
belt incline and decline	运输带
live roller	活动滚筒
sorter and divert	分拣机
waste processing conveyor	废物运输机

Notes（注释）

In detail, it is a large and automated center designated to receive goods from various plants and suppliers, take orders, fill orders efficiently, and deliver goods to customers on time. 具体的说，配送中心是一个大型的自动化中心，它从工厂和供应者手中接受货物，接受订单，有效执行订单，并将货物准时送给客户。

Dialogue Two

A Distribution Agreement(销售协议)

(Mr. Huang, leader of a food factory, is talking with Mr. Gross, a British importer.)

H: Mr. Gross. Welcome to our factory. Please take a seat.

G: Thank you.

H: Did you have a look around our factory?

G: Yes, I did. I think people in your factory are very friendly and the management is well-ordered.

H: Thanks.

G: We used to buy your food products through the export corporations. Now we are happy to be able to deal with you directly.

H: So are we.

G: You will be able to secure a steady flow of export orders if you can conclude a distribution agreement with us.

H: A distribution agreement?

G: Yes. If you appoint us as your distributor of food products in our area, then we will undertake not to buy them from any other sources.

H: And we shall not sell directly to other customers in your area.

G: Right. And we will undertake to place orders with you in a fixed time. This way you needn't worry about the credit of the buyers in this area. As you know, our credit and commercial standing are well known to many people.

H: This is true, yet we need time to know each other especially the way of doing business.

G: I agree with you.

Words and Phrases(单词与短语)

secure /si'kjuə/		v. 获得,紧握
steady /'stedi/		adj. 稳定的
conclude /kən'klu:d/		v. 决定
appoint /ə'pɔint/		v. 委派,指定
undertake /ˌʌndə'teik/		v. 承诺,保证
well-ordered		秩序井然的
the credit of the buyers		买方的信用度
place order		订购
credit and commercial standing		信用和商务地位

Notes(注释)

1. You will be able to secure a steady flow of export orders if you can conclude a distribution agreement with us. 如果你能与我们签订销售协议,你将能获得稳定的出口预订量。

2. If you appoint us as your distributor of food products in our area, then we will undertake not to buy them from any other sources. 如果你指定我们在这个区域是你们食品的批发商,那么我们保证不从其他货源购买食品。

Knowledge accumulation(知识积累)

1. The distribution center provides the customer with perfect and efficient service. 配送中心为客户提供高水平、高效率的服务。

2. Order picking refers to picking up the destined goods according to the orders.
订单分拣指的是根据订单收集指定货物。

3. Sorting refers to putting the goods into separated package according to the order.
分类指的是根据订单将货物进行不同的包装。

 Exercises（练习）

1. Translate the following phrases/sentences into Chinese/English（英汉互译）.

1) order processing　　　　　　　　　　_____

2) storage distribution center　　　　　_____

3) value-added activities　　　　　　　_____

4) 实时数据　　　　　　　　　　　　　_____

5) 订单分拣　　　　　　　　　　　　　_____

6) 快递配送　　　　　　　　　　　　　_____

7) Waste processing conveyors are one of the units of distribution center.

_____

8) Can you conclude a distribution agreement with us now?

_____

9) 让我们一起去参观一个配送中心吧！

_____

10) 别担心买方的信用度。

_____

2. Answer the following questions in English（回答问题）.

1) What is distribution center?

_____

2) What basic function do the distribution centers have?

_____

3) What steps do operation flow of distribution have?

_____

4) How did Mr. Gross used to buy food products from Mr. Huang in Dialogue Two?

_____

3. Choose the best answers according to description（选择题）.

(　　)1) Distribution center is a logistics link to fulfill（履行）physical _____ as its main function.

　　　　A. transport　　　B. handling　　　C. distribution　　　D. movement

(　　)2) Distribution center performs a great deal of _____ activities, such as packaging, labeling(贴标签), etc.

　　　　A. value-added　　B. useful　　　C. important　　　D. difficult

(　　)3) Distribution centers are highly _____ places to receive goods from various plants and suppliers.

  A. modern   B. automated   C. poor   D. progressive

( )4) Distribution centers provide the _____ with perfect and efficient service level（高水平、高效率的服务）.

  A. sellers   B. buyers   C. users   D. customers

( )5) DCs collect _____ in real time.

  A. goods   B. people   C. data   D. financial

( )6) If you appoint us your distributor of food products in our area, then we will undertake _____ them from any other sources.

  A. buy   B. not to buy   C. sell   D. not sell

( )7) Timely distribution means _____.

  A. 及时配送   B. 定时配送   C. 按时配送   D. 定路线配送

( )8) _____ is located close to a major market in logistics.

  A. Warehouse   B. Port

  C. Distribution center   D. Goods

( )9) Tack: Which one is not the equipment in DC?

  Jane: _____.

  A. Declines   B. Live rollers

  C. Sorters   D. Washing machine

( )10) Kate: Is the value-added service(VAS) preparation area one of the functional areas of the distribution center?

  Han Fei: _____.

  A. No   B. Yes

  C. No, I think so   D. Yes, I'm not sure

4. **Reading passage（阅读小短文）.**

Maersk Logistics Opened National Distribution Center

  Maersk Logistics China opened a large National Distribution Center（NDC）in Jiuting Town in Shanghai in mid June. Chinese government officials including Zhou Xuedi, Deputy Magistrate of Songjiang District（松江区副区长）, Liu Weizhong, Deputy Magistrate of Huangpu District, and officials from Jiuting Town attended the opening ceremony（开幕式）, which was inaugurated by Tom Behrens Sorensen（由 Behrens 主持了落成仪式）, President of Maersk China Shipping Co. Ltd.

  The new Maersk Logistics facility（设施）is about 14,000 sqm large and is located in the Jiuting economic development zone（经济开发区）of Songjiang District, an ideal location（理想场所）for an integrated logistics center in Shanghai. The NDC is conveniently connected to Shanghai's outer expressway, providing easy access to and from key ports, roads and other distribution channels for importers, local manufacturers and exporters.

  The new NDC will offer the customers specialized supply chain management services including cross docking（直接换装）, putting in storage, sorting（分拣）, importing, exporting, and distributing in China. In addition（另外）, with the state-of-the-art IT system（信息系统技术）Maersk Logistics will ensure（确保）the efficiency of supply chain, inventory and warehouse management.

The distribution center is an important leg in Pan-china Distribution Network of Maersk Logistics China which is rapidly expanding. Maersk Logistics China has its head office in Shanghai, with nine branches（分支）and five representative offices（办事处）across the country.

根据短文内容选择问题最合适的答语。

(   )1) Tom: Where is the National Distribution Center of Maersk Logistics China located?
Jane: _____.
A. Beijing   B. Guangzhou   C. Shanghai   D. Tianjing

(   )2) Tom: What will the new NDC offer?
Jane: _____.
A. Storage   B. Import   C. Distribution   D. All above

(   )3) Tom: How many representative offices are there across the country?
Jane: _____.
A. Nine   B. Five   C. One   D. None.

Unit Five
Transportation

Part One Learning Target (学习目标)

1. To know the importance and functions of transportation.
2. To know the basic modes of transportation.
3. To develop communication skills in talking about transportation.

Part Two Learning Contents (学习内容)

Text One

What is Transportation? (运输是什么?)

1. The Importance of Transportation (运输的重要性)

Transportation usually is the most important single element in logistics activity for most firms. Thus, the logistician needs a good understanding of transportation matters.

Logistics involves the movement of products (raw materials, parts, and finished goods) from point-of-origin to point-of-consumption. A product has very little value to the prospective customer unless it is moved to the point where it will be consumed. Transportation fulfils this movement.

Transportation creates value. It determines how fast a product moves from one point to another point. This is known as time-in-transit. If a product is not available when needed, the company will probably miss the chance to sale, and the customer may feel very disappointed.

2. Modes of Transportation (运输的方式)

There are five transportation modes—motor, rail, air, water, and pipeline. In addition, certain mode combinations are available, including rail-motor, motor-water, motor-air, and rail-water. Such combinations offer special or lower cost services, but they are not generally as available as a single transport mode.

  motor   pipeline   water   air   rail

Words and Phrases(单词与短语)

element /ˈelimənt/	n. 要素,成分
firm /fəːm/	n. 公司,商行
logistician /ləˈdʒistiʃən/	n. 物流技术员,物流工程师
understanding /ˌʌndəˈstændiŋ/	n. 了解,认识
consumption /kənˈsʌmpʃən/	n. 消费;消耗
create /kriˈeit/	v. 创造,产生
dissatisfaction /disˌsætisˈfækʃən/	n. 失望,失落
combination /ˌkɔmbiˈneiʃən/	n. 联合;结合
loss /lɔs/	n. 损失,亏损
mode /məud/	n. 形式,模式
logistics activity	物流活动
raw materials	原材料
finished goods	成品
in addition	另外

Notes(注释)

1. If a product is not available when needed, the company will probably miss the chance to sale, and the customer may feel very disappointed. 如果不能及时提供顾客所需要的商品,企业很可能会错失销售良机,同时令顾客大失所望。

2. Such combinations offer special or lower cost services, but they are not generally as available as a single transport mode. 联合运输形式能够提供特殊的或者更廉价的运输服务,但它们并不像单一运输方式那么容易实现。

Unit Five
Transportation

Dialogue One

Let Apples Make More Money(让苹果挣更多的钱)

(*Jane owns a farm. It is in good harvest this year. Jane has done a big deal.*)

Tom: You look very happy. What happened to you?
Jane: Guess.
Tom: Jane. Come on, what happened to you?
Jane: My lovely apples have been sold at a good price.
Tom: How did you make it?
Jane: I sold them to the downtown.
Tom: What is the difference between selling in the downtown and in its origin place?
Jane: There are more people need these goods in the downtown.
Tom: It sounds very interesting. Could you tell me more? I can't wait.
Jane: No hurry. I'll let you know the process sooner or later.

Words and Phrases (单词与短语)

harvest /ˈhɑːvist/	n.	收获,收成
deal /diːl/	n.	交易,买卖
guess /ges/	n.	猜测,推测
lovely /ˈlʌvli/	a.	可爱的,美好的
downtown /ˌdaunˈtaun/	n.	城市商业区
origin /ˈɔridʒin/	n.	产地

Notes (注释)

There are more people need these goods in the downtown. 商业区有更多的人需要这一类的货品(商业区有更多的消费者)。

Text Two

Functions of Transportation(运输功能)

Transportation fulfils different functions:
1. Contributes to creating a high level of living. Because of available transportation

services, all kinds of products could be sent to the places where more people need them and the average economic standard of people's living rises.

2. Contributes to increasing competition in the market. With improvement in the transportation system, the products from distant areas can be competitive with other local products.

3. Contributes to reducing production costs. An efficient transportation system could bring more cheaper materials from different places, which leads to a lower production cost. With the expanding of markets, production facilities are used more often, the specialization division of labor is getting more obvious.

4. Contributes to reducing product prices. Transportation cost, along with production, selling, and other distribution costs compose the aggregate product cost.

   waterway   railway   pipeline   road   air sign

 ## Words and Phrases (单词与短语)

available /əˈveiləbl/	a. 可用的,可得到的
average /ˈævəridʒ/	adj. 平均的
economic /ˌikəˈnɔmik/	adj. 经济的
standard /ˈstændəd/	n. 标准,平均质量
rise /raiz/	vi. 升高,上涨,增加
compose /kəmˈpəuz/	vt. 构成,组成
competition /ˌkɔmpəˈtiʃən/	n. 竞争,比赛
specialization /ˌspeʃəlaiˈzeiʃən/	n. 专业化,专门化
distribution /ˌdistriˈbjuːʃən/	n. 流通,分销
aggregate /ˈægrigət/	a. 合计的;总的
efficient /iˈfiʃənt/	a. 效率高的;有能力的

 ## Notes (注释)

1. With improvement in the transportation system, the products from distant areas can be competitive with other local products. 随着运输系统的不断完善,远道而来的商品同样能够跟当地的商品进行有力的市场竞争。

2. With the expanding of markets, production facilities are used more often, the

specialization division of labor is getting more obvious. 在市场空间和容量不断扩大的同时,生产设备的使用率不断地提高,劳动力的专业化分工也越趋明显。

Dialogue Two

How Do Apples Make More Money?(苹果怎样挣更多的钱?)

Tom: Can you make more money through changing the place of selling?

Jane: Absolutely, transportation helps me accomplish the task.

Tom: Could you explain it to me?

Jane: With my pleasure.

Tom: I am listening.

Jane: Price depends on demand. There are more people living in downtown. More people generate more demand, and then the price will rise.

Tom: Oh, I really see. Through transportation, the changing of place can increase the value of goods. Good idea! How did you come up with this idea?

Jane: It comes from my teacher. Remember: An old Chinese saying goes that frequent shifts make a tree dead but make a person prosperous. Sometimes selling goods is just the same.

 Words and Phrases(单词与短语)

absolutely /ˈæbsəˌluːtli/	adv. 完全地,当然
transportation /ˌtrænspɔːˈteiʃən/	n. 运输
accomplish /əˈkʌmpliʃ/	v. 完成,实现
task /tɑːsk/	n. 任务,工作
explain /ikˈsplein/	v. 解释,说明
generate /ˈdʒenəreit/	v. 产生,引起
think up	想起,想到
place of selling	销售地
increase the value	增值

 Notes(注释)

1. Absolutely, transportation helps me accomplish the task. 当然了,运输能够帮助我完成这个业务。

2. Price depends on demand. There are more people living in downtown. More people

generate more demand, and then the price will rise. 价格取决于需求。商业区的人口量要比产地的多。人口多,需求量也会大,价格自然就会上涨。

3. An old Chinese saying goes that frequent shifts make a tree dead but make a person prosperous. 中国有一句古话:人挪活,树挪死。

 Knowledge accumulation（知识积累）

1. Transportation is a vital component in the design and management of logistics systems. 运输是物流系统设计和管理中至关重要的组成部分。

2. Pipelines can work twenty-four hours per day basis, seven days per week, we only need to change the products and take necessary maintenance. 管道可以一周七天、一天二十四小时运作,只需要更换运输的产品和进行必要的维修保养。

3. Water carriage is particularly suited for movement of heavy, bulky, low-value-per-unit commodities. 水运特别适合于重的、大量的、单位价值低的货物。

4. The main disadvantages of water transport are the limited range and speed of transport. 水路运输的主要缺点是运输范围和速度受到限制。

5. Freight rates are based on three factors: distance, shipment condition and competition. 运费主要取决于运输距离、装运条件和竞争三种因素。

6. There are two types of shipping markets: the liner market and the tramp market. 航运市场分为两类:班轮运输和不定期船运输。

7. Air transportation is increasing, it is the best choice for certain goods, such as fresh food or flowers as well as valuables. 空运业务不断增长,它是某些商品如新鲜食品、鲜花以及贵重物品的最佳选择。

 Exercises（练习）

1. Translate the following phrases/sentences into Chinese/English(英汉互译).

1) 运输　　　　　　　　　　　＿＿＿＿＿＿＿＿＿＿＿＿＿＿＿＿

2) 物流活动　　　　　　　　　＿＿＿＿＿＿＿＿＿＿＿＿＿＿＿＿

3) transportation mode　　　　＿＿＿＿＿＿＿＿＿＿＿＿＿＿＿＿

4) point of consumption　　　　＿＿＿＿＿＿＿＿＿＿＿＿＿＿＿＿

5) customer　　　　　　　　　＿＿＿＿＿＿＿＿＿＿＿＿＿＿＿＿

6) 物流技术员　　　　　　　　＿＿＿＿＿＿＿＿＿＿＿＿＿＿＿＿

7) Wider markets result from an efficient and inexpensive transportation lead to a lower production cost.

＿＿＿＿＿＿＿＿＿＿＿＿＿＿＿＿＿＿＿＿＿＿＿＿＿＿＿＿＿＿＿＿＿＿＿＿＿＿＿

＿＿＿＿＿＿＿＿＿＿＿＿＿＿＿＿＿＿＿＿＿＿＿＿＿＿＿＿＿＿＿＿＿＿＿＿＿＿＿

8) 对于大部分的企业来说,运输是物流活动中最重要的部分。

9) A product has very little value to the prospective customer unless it is moved to the point where it will be consumed.

10) 一共有五种运输方式——汽车运输、铁路运输、航空运输、水路运输以及管道运输。

2. Answer the following questions in English(回答问题).

1) How do you think of the role of transportation in logistics activity?

2) If you are a logistician, what should you do?

3) How does transportation create value?

4) How does transportation contribute to creating a high level economic activity?

3. Choose the best answers according to description(选择题).

(　　)1) How to make a product more valuable through transportation?
　　　A. To change the position of product.
　　　B. To change the figure of product.
　　　C. To change the package of product.
　　　D. To change the name of product.

(　　)2) Is transportation critical in logistics activity?
　　　A. Yes.　　　　　　　　　　B. No.
　　　C. Not mentioned.　　　　　D. Obscure.

(　　)3) Why does a logistician need a good understanding of transportation matters?
　　　A. Because he/she does a study.
　　　B. Because he/she loves the position deeply.
　　　C. Because he/she is a driver.
　　　D. Because he/she should improve the transportation system.

(　　)4) If a product is not available when needed, what would happen to the customers?
　　　A. The company would make more money.
　　　B. The customers would be disappointed.
　　　C. The price of products would be much higher.
　　　D. Market share would be suffering.

(　　)5) How many transportation modes mentioned in the first paragraph?
　　　A. Four.　　　B. Five.　　　C. Six.　　　D. Seven.

(　　)6) Is modes combination more available than single transport mode?
　　　A. Yes.　　　　　　　　　B. No.
　　　C. Not mentioned　　　　 D. Obscure

(　　)7) How many functions does transportation fulfil?
　　　A. Four.　　　B. Five.　　　C. Six.　　　D. Seven.

(　　)8) An efficient and inexpensive transportation may make the price of products _____.
　　　A. lower　　　　　　　　B. higher
　　　C. stable　　　　　　　　D. fluctuant

(　　)9) The expanding of markets is accompany with _____ of products.
　　　A. lower cost　　　　　　B. higher cost
　　　C. promotion　　　　　　D. fluctuation

(　　)10) Which factor most affect the structure of economy in a nation?
　　　A. Warehousing.　　　　B. Packaging.
　　　C. Transportation.　　　　D. Handling.

4. Reading passage(阅读小短文).

There are five transportation modes: rail, highway, water, pipeline and air.

1) Rail network. Rail network can be used to transport large tonnage goods over long distance. Rail company has the advantage of low operation cost on electricity and fuel, and the disadvantage of expensive investment.

2) Motor carriers. Highway transport has developed rapidly since 1970. The operation of door-to-door and its flexibility are the main reasons why other modes can't be compared with motor carries.

3) Water transport. Water transport is the oldest way of transportation, but it is the only one for international trading. Ocean ships can sail very long distance and carry extremely large shipments with the lowest cost. Recently, container ship may load 7000 containers weighed about 150000 tons.

4) Pipeline. Pipeline can send goods without stopping, but goods are restricted to oil and gas. In 2003, China began to build three pipelines for water transportation calls "South-to-North water diversion".

5) Air. Air freights is the newest and sun rise industry. Although it is high cost now, in a long run, air transport will increase its proportion steadily.

根据短文内容选择问题最合适的答语。

(　　)1) Tom: Which is the most widespread way of transportation used in international trading?
　　　　Jane: _____.
　　　A. Rail　　　B. Highway　　　C. Water　　　D. Air

(   )2) Tom: Which is the youngest way of transportation?

   Jane:_____.

   A. Rail   B. Highway   C. Water   D. Air

(   )3) Tom: Which is more qualified to be a low-carbon way of transportation comparing with other ones?

   Jane:_____.

   A. Rail   B. Highway   C. Water   D. Air

Unit Six
International Logistics

Part One Learning Target (学习目标)

1. To understand the trends in international logistics.
2. To know some intermediaries of international logistics.
3. To acquire knowledge about containers.
4. To develop the communication skill in talking about logistics and unloading.

Part Two Learning Contents (学习内容)

Text One

Trends in International Logistics(国际物流未来趋势)

As global trade increases, almost every company in the world is involved in international trade to some extent. The requirement to increase or maintain profits and sales pushes so many firms into global markets. International trade is growing rapidly and will continue to increase at an even faster rate. So in the future, companies need to develop more integrated logistics system to move the products across national boundaries, to improve more networked management, to reach more unified standard, to perform finer delivery, to build more convenient garden area and to achieve more modernized logistics.

Challenges of International Logistics(国际物流面对的挑战)

Global integrated logistics activities differ from domestic integrated logistics. The following aspects deserve special attention: transportation, warehouse management, packaging, inventory management, material handling, and information systems. In addition, response time, the completeness and accuracy to fulfil an order, and shipment condition demand particular attention from the global logistics managers.

One challenge is that response time in international logistics is usually longer because of longer distance, slower movement by sea freight, and more documentation. The uncertainty in the time taken to undertake international transport will inevitably lead to the increase of inventory with the aim of avoiding short of stock in retail markets. As the lead time increases, some companies may face the situation of being out of stock. So they often carry larger inventories to minimize stock-outs. It will cause higher holding or carrying costs.

Another challenge is the consignees may often change their requirements. Thus much more time will be needed to fulfil their orders completely and accurately. There is one last point we need to pay attention, when a large number of intermediaries are involved in global logistics, the safety of goods becomes particularly important. Any loss, damage, or theft will bring additional cost.

 Words and Phrases (单词与短语)

maintain /meinˈtein/	v. 保持
profit /ˈprɔfit/	n. 利润
integrated /ˈintiɡreitid/	adj. 集成的, 连成一体的
networked /ˈnetwəːkt/	adj. 网络化的
unified /ˈjuːnifaid/	adj. 统一化的
perform /pəˈfɔːm/	v. 执行, 履行
convenient /kənˈviːniənt/	adj. 便利的
modernized /ˈmɔdəˌnaizd/	adj. 现代化的
involve in	参与
to some extent	或多或少
at an even faster rate	以更快的速度
across national boundaries	不同国界之间

 Notes (注释)

1. to develop more integrated logistics system to move the products across national boundaries 建立一个集成化的物流系统使得货物能畅通于不同国界之间

2. Global integrated logistics activities differ from domestic integrated logistics. The following aspects deserve special attention: transportation, warehouse management, packaging, inventory management, material handling, and information systems. In addition, response time, the completeness and accuracy to fulfil an order, and shipment condition demand particular attention from the global logistics managers. 全球整合的物流活动跟只在国内整合的物流活动有很大的分别。下面这些环节需要特别的关注，运输、仓储管理、包装、库存管理、原料处理、信息系统。额外地，反应时间、订单履行的完整性和准确性、收发货物的情况等这些指标都要求国际物流经理们加以特别的关注。

3. One challenge is that response time in international logistics is usually longer because of longer distance, slower movement by sea freight, and more documentation. The uncertainty in the time taken to undertake international transport will inevitably lead to the increase of inventory with the aim of avoiding short of stock in retail markets. As the lead time increases, some companies may face the situation of being out of stock. So they often carry larger inventories to minimize stock-outs. It will cause higher holding or carrying costs. 一个风险就是国际间物流运作的反应时间通常会因为运输距离长、海运的速度慢以及烦琐的各种文件等因素变得更长。所以，为了避免零售终端缺货的情况，在国际运输中各种时间的不确定性都会不可避免地导致存货的增加。由于交付周期变长，一些公司将面临缺货的局面，所以他们经常加大库存以使缺货。

4. Another challenge is the consignees may often change their requirements. Thus much more time will be needed to fulfil their orders completely and accurately. There is one last point we need to pay attention, when a large number of intermediaries are involved in global logistics, the safety of goods becomes particularly important. Any loss, damage, or theft will bring additional cost. 另一个风险是收货人经常会修改他们的订单，使得要完整而及时地满足他们要求的订单处理时间变得更长。最后值得注意的是，因为有许多代理人及操作者加入到国际物流的活动中来，对货物安全的考虑变得尤为重要，遗失、破损、被盗等都会产生额外的成本。

Dialogue One

Changing the Port of Unloading(改变卸货港)

(This is a conversation between Tom, the manager in a logistics company and Jane, a customer of the company.)

Tom: Jane, are you tired today after visiting Guangzhou yesterday?

Jane: No, not at all. Guangzhou is very beautiful. I am very interested in Guangzhou.

Tom: Great! Let's discuss the port of unloading then.

Jane: I'm all ready.

Tom: Our offer is CIF American main ports. The time of shipment is May. What's your unloading port, please?

Jane: Houston.

Tom: Houston? Sorry. In May, there isn't any shipment to Houston. How about New York?

Jane: As you know, most of our customers are near Houston. It's not reasonable to unload the goods at New York.

Tom: I see.

Jane: We hope you'll contact the shipping company once again to make sure that the shipment will arrive in Houston.

Tom: I am sure to do that, there is a ship sailing to Houston in June. But I'm afraid it's too late to book the shipping space.

Jane: Please try your best, and I believe that you can do it well.

Tom: I'll certainly try my best.

Jane: Thanks. Hope we'll have a pleasant cooperation.

Words and Phrases（单词与短语）

port /pɔːt/	n. 港口
unload /ʌnˈləud/	v. 卸货
offer /ˈɔfə/	n. 报价
shipment /ˈʃipmənt/	n. （经海路、陆路或航空运送的）货物
Houston /ˈhjuːstən/	n. 休斯敦
reasonable /ˈriːzənəbl/	adj. 合理的
contact /ˈkɔntækt/	v. 联系
cooperation /kəuˌɔpəˈreiʃən/	n. 合作
CIF (Cost, Insurance and Freight)	到岸价（成本、保险加运费）
the shipping company	船运公司
book the shipping space	预订仓位

Notes（注释）

We hope you'll contact the shipping company once again to make sure that the shipment will arrive in Houston. 我们希望你将再一次联系船运公司确保装载的货物将达到休斯敦。

Global Intermediaries of International Logistics(国际物流的中介)

Because international logistics is complex, a global company will adopt logistics strategy to manage the across-border logistics. The across-border logistics need to use Third-Party Logistics providers. They are also known as the Intermediaries of International logistics. Third-Party Logistics offers specialists to help with the export/import transaction. They play an important role in the global integrated logistics process.

Common types of global intermediaries include international freight forwarders, customs brokers, shipping agents and export management companies.

1. International Freight Forwarders: They consolidate small shipments into full loads and disperse them. They operate as either air or water freight forwarders.

2. Customs Brokers: They facilitate the movement of goods through customs.

3. Shipping Agents: They are local representatives of ship operators. They assist in berthing the ship, clearance, loading and unloading the vessel.

4. Export Management Companies: They market a company's products globally, acting as professional exporters. They perform important functions such as getting orders, choosing the distribution channels, warehousing space, and overseeing inventory.

customs sign

Words and Phrases (单词与短语)

intermediary /ˌɪntəˈmiːdiəri/	n. 中间人
complex /ˈkɔmpleks/	adj. 复杂的
global /ˈɡləubəl/	adj. 全球的
adopt /əˈdɔpt/	v. 采用
strategy /ˈstrætidʒi/	n. 战略
provider /prəˈvaidə/	n. 供应者
specialist /ˈspeʃəlist/	n. 专家,服务商

transaction /trænˈzækʃən/	n. 处理,协助
disperse /diˈspəːs/	v. 驱散,分散
manage the across-border logistic	管理跨境的物流业务
Third-Party Logistic	第三方物流
international freight forwarder	国际货运公司
customs broker	海关报关公司
shipping agent	船运代理公司
local representative	当地代理人

Notes（注释）

1. They play an important role in the global integrated logistics process. 他们在整条国际物流链中起到关键的作用。

2. They consolidate small shipments into full loads and disperse them. 他们将货物进行汇集或分散。

3. They facilitate the movement of goods through customs. 他们帮助顾客完成货物通过海关的各种手续。

4. They assist in berthing the ship, clearance, loading and unloading the vessel. 他们协助客户安排货船的停泊港、处理清关工作及货物的装卸工作。

5. They market a company's products globally, acting as professional exporters. 他们作为一个专业的出口商为客户的产品进行全球管理。

Dialogue Two

Knowing about Containers（了解集装箱）

(*Miss Wang is an agent of a shipping company. Mr. Smith is a clerk of an American logistics company.*)

Wang: Welcome to our company. I am Wang Lin. Can I help you?

Smith: Good afternoon, Miss Wang. I'm here for the information about containers.

Wang: Do you want to book containers?

Smith: Yes, I'm quite interested in containers. I wonder what size of containers you'll load our goods with.

Wang: We have twenty-foot equivalent units and forty-foot containers. Which one do you prefer?

Smith: Could you tell me what your containers are made of?

Wang: No problem. They are made of metal and are of standard lengths from 10 to 40 feet.

Smith: Then I'll choose TEUs.

Wang: All right. You know the advantages of the containers, don't you?

Smith: Of course. Using the containers reduces not only the time and manpower of handling and loading, but also costs and risk of losing and damaging the goods.

Wang: You are right. When would you like to sign contract with us?

Smith: Right now.

Wang: I think it's a good beginning for us.

Smith: So I do.

Words and Phrases（单词与短语）

agent /ˈeidʒənt/	n. 代理人
clerk /klɑːk/	n. 职员
container /kənˈteinə/	n. 集装箱
equivalent /iˈkwivələnt/	adj. 相等的，相当的
advantage /ədˈvɑːntidʒ/	n. 优势
reduce /riˈdjuːs/	v. 减少，降低
risk /risk/	n. 风险
damage /ˈdæmidʒ/	v. 损害
have any connection with	与……有关
TEUs(20-food equivalent units)	20 英尺(1 英尺＝0.3048 米)的标箱

Notes（注释）

1. We have twenty-foot equivalent units and forty-foot containers. 我们有 20 英尺的标箱和 40 英尺的集装箱。

2. Using the containers reduces not only the time and manpower of handling and loading, but also costs and risk of losing and damaging the goods. 使用集装箱不仅减少搬运和装货的时间和人力，而且降低成本，还降低货物丢失和损坏的风险。

Knowledge accumulation（知识积累）

1. Maritime shipping is an important link of international logistics service. 海洋运输是国

际物流服务的重要环节。

2. A Container Load Plan is of five copies, which are separately given to the terminal, the carrier, the shipping agent, the shipper and the party that stuffs the container. 集装箱装箱单一式五份,分别交给集装箱码头、承运人、船务代理、托运人和装箱人。

3. After the cargo is stuffed into a container, it is carried to the container yard (CY) and then loaded on board according to the stowage plan. 货物装箱后,就拖运到集装箱堆场并根据积载图装上船。

4. A container terminal connects sea and land, transferring containers to and from ships. It is capable of handling containers more quickly, economically, accurately and in greater volumes than conventional ports. 集装箱码头连接陆运和海运,经船上装运集装箱。在装卸搬运上,集装箱码头比普通杂货码头更快、更经济、更准确、吞吐量更大。

Exercises(练习)

1. Translate the following phrases/sentences into Chinese/English(英汉互译).

1) international logistics　　　　_____
2) the port of unloading　　　　_____
3) perform finer delivery　　　　_____
4) 预订仓位　　　　　　　　　　_____
5) 到岸价　　　　　　　　　　　_____
6) 标箱　　　　　　　　　　　　_____
7) Nowadays, many firms have to enter global markets.
_____

8) With the increasing of international trade, we cooperate with Third-Party Logistics more often.
_____

9) 我们需要找一个国际货运公司。
_____

10) 在国际贸易运输中,人们使用集装箱装载货物。
_____

2. Answer the following questions in English(回答问题).

1) What does Tom do in Dialogue One?
_____

2) What are Tom and Jane talking about?
_____

3) Is a container heavy or light, what do you think?
_____

4) How many common types do global intermediaries have?
_____

3. Choose the best answers according to description(选择题).

(　　)1) Li: What are Tom and Jane talking about in Dialogue One?
　　　　Wang: _____.
　　　　A. The port of loading　　　　B. The port of unloading
　　　　C. Containers　　　　　　　　D. Documents

(　　)2) Hu: What does CIF means?
　　　　Wu: Costs, _____ and Freight.
　　　　A. Internal　　　　　　　　　B. Inland
　　　　C. Insurance　　　　　　　　D. International

(　　)3) Li: What feature do containers have in the transportation of international trading?
　　　　Wang: They are made of _____ and are of standard _____.
　　　　A. wood, lengths　　　　　　B. metal, long
　　　　C. metal, lengths　　　　　　D. wood, long

(　　)4) A full container load(整箱服务) and less than a full container load(拼箱服务) may be written as _____ and _____ for short.
　　　　A. AFCL, LTFCL　　　　　　B. FCL, LTFC
　　　　C. AFCL, LCL　　　　　　　D. FCL, LCL

(　　)5) Gong: Why is response time usually longer in international logistics?
　　　　Ji: Because of _____.
　　　　A. distance　　　　　　　　B. movement
　　　　C. documentation　　　　　D. All of above.

(　　)6) Wu: Is international logistics complex?
　　　　Li: _____.
　　　　A. No　　　　　　　　　　　B. Yes
　　　　C. I am not sure　　　　　　D. I don't think so

(　　)7) _____ Logistics offers specialists(特别经纪人) to help with the export/import transaction(事务).
　　　　A. Third-Party　　　　　　　B. International
　　　　C. Local　　　　　　　　　　D. Global

(　　)8) With the increasing of international _____, many firms have entered global markets.
　　　　A. system　　B. business　　C. trade　　D. containers

(　　)9) Customs brokers facilitate the movement of goods through _____.
　　　　A. customs　　　　　　　　B. insurance company
　　　　C. market　　　　　　　　　D. system

(　　)10) Tom: What freight forwarders do International Freight Forwarders operate as?
　　　　Cheng: Either _____ or water.

A. land　　　　　B. air　　　　　C. pipeline　　　　D. \

4. Reading passage(阅读小对话).

A：Hello. Welcome.

B：Can I speak to Mike Chen?

A：Speaking.

B：This is Guangming Electronics Co.（电子公司）of Guangzhou.

A：Have you received the request（请求）from the Guangzhou Customs House（海关）regarding（关于）the survey of your cargo?

B：Yes. But is it a condition to go through the customs clearance procedures（通关程序）?

A：Yes, of course. The Customs House must make sure that the goods you sent to be exported conform to（符合）what is stated（规定的）on the airway bill.

B：But the consignment is very small, only 100 kilograms of CDs.

A：It is the rule that each and every consignment for export will be inspected（检查）before leaving China.

B：Can't you put in a word for us? You are our freight forwarder for so many years and....

A：Sorry. But that is the rules of the game. You had better send someone here as soon as possible. Otherwise, warehousing expense（仓储费用）will incur（引起）.

B：OK. Xiao Wang from our export department will be with you this afternoon.

A：I will be in my office then. Bye-bye.

B：Bye-bye.

根据对话内容选择问题最合适的答语。

(　　)1) Jack：What does Mike Chen do?

　　　　　Jane：_____.

　　　　　A. A shipper　　　　　　　　B. A manager

　　　　　C. A freight forwarder　　　　D. A carrier

(　　)2) Jack：Why Guangming Electronics Co. of Guangzhou does not want the consignment be inspected?

　　　　　Jane：Because the consignment is very _____.

　　　　　A. big　　　　B. small　　　　C. heavy　　　　D. old

(　　)3) Jack：Will any consignment for exporter be inspected?

　　　　　Jane：_____.

　　　　　A. Yes　　　　　　　　　　　B. No

　　　　　C. No mentioned　　　　　　D. I don't think so

Unit Seven
Logistics Documents

Part One Learning Target (学习目标)

1. To develop the skill in writing business letters.
2. To grasp how to use the B/L.
3. To understand some main documents in logistics.
4. To know the functions of some logistics documents.

Part Two Learning Contents (学习内容)

Text One

Introduction of Logistics Documents(物流单证的介绍)

Types of Logistics Documents(物流单证类型)

Logistics documents refer to all documents involved in the course of logistics. According to the source of documents, there are three kinds of commonly used logistics documents. They are government documents, commercial documents and transport documents.

1. Government documents include import/export license, customs declaration form, inspection certificate, certificate of origin, generalized system of preferences certificate of origin (form A) customs declaration entrustment note, export tax rebate form and foreign exchange cancellation-after-verification note.

2. Commercial documents include bill of exchange or draft, insurance policy, commercial invoice, packing list, customs invoice, consular invoice, beneficiary's statement, shipping advice, captain receipt, itinerary certificate, certificate of sample, beneficiary's certificate, credit note, debit note and letter of credit(L/C).

3. Transport documents include shipper's letter of instruction, space booking note,

shipping order(S/O), mate's receipt, packing list, container shipping note, dock receipt, container load plan(CLP), bill of lading(B/L)(MB/L & HB/L, sea waybill), combined transport B/L, delivery order(D/O), equipment interchange receipt, railway bill, road waybill, cargo receipt(C/R), cargo manifest, cargo plan, master air waybill(MAWB), house air waybill, and forwarder's certificate of receipt(FCR).

 Words and Phrases(单词与短语)

declaration /ˌdekləˈreiʃən/	n. 申报
inspection /inˈspekʃən/	n. 检查
certificate /səˈtifikət/	n. 证书
generalized /ˈdʒenrəlaizd/	adj. 普遍的
preference /ˈprefərəns/	n. 优惠
entrustment /inˈtrʌstmənt/	n. 委托
rebate /ˈriːbeit/	n. 退款
cancellation /ˌkænsəˈleiʃən/	n. 注销
verification /ˌverifiˈkeiʃən/	n. 证明
draft /drɑːft/	n. 汇票
consular /ˈkɔnsjələ/	adj. 领事的
beneficiary /ˌbeniˈfiʃəriː/	n. 受益者
government document	官方单证
commercial document	商业单证
transport document	运输单证

 Notes(注释)

1. Government documents include import/export license, customs declaration form, inspection certificate, certificate of origin, generalized system of preferences certificate of origin (form A), customs declaration entrustment note, export tax rebate form and foreign exchange cancellation-after-verification note. 官方单证包括进/出口许可证、报关单、商检证、原产地证明、惠普制产地证(表格 A)、报关委托书、出口退税单和外汇核销单。

2. Commercial documents include bill of exchange or draft, insurance policy, commercial invoice, packing list, customs invoice, consular invoice, beneficiary's statement, shipping advice, captain receipt, itinerary certificate, certificate of sample, beneficiary's certificate, credit note, debit note and letter of credit(L/C). 商业单证包括汇票、保险单、商业发票、装箱单、海关发票、领事发票、寄单证明、装船通知、船长收据、航程证明、寄样证明、受益人证明、贷记证明、借记证明和信用证。

3. Transport documents include shipper's letter of instruction, space booking note, shipping order(S/O), mate's receipt, packing list, container shipping note, dock receipt,

container load plan(CLP), bill of lading(B/L)(MB/L & HB/L, sea waybill), combined transport B/L, delivery order(D/O), equipment interchange receipt, railway bill, road waybill, cargo receipt(C/R), cargo manifest, cargo plan, master air waybill(MAWB), house air waybill, and forwarder's certificate of receipt(FCR). 运输单证包括出口货物代运委托书、订舱单、装货单、收货单(大副收据)、装箱单、托运单、集装箱场站收据、集装箱装货单、海运提单(主提单与分提单,海运单)、(多式)联运提单、提货单(交货单)、设备交接单、铁路运单、陆路运单、承运货物收据、舱单、货物积载图、航空主单、航空分单和发运代理收据。

Dialogue One

Knowing the Business Letters(了解商务信函)

(*The following is a conversation between Li Yang, a student majoring in logistics and Wang Ying, a logistics teacher.*)

Wang: Good morning, everyone! Let's begin our class.

Li & Ss: Good morning, Mrs. Wang!

Wang: Today we will learn how to write a business letter. Who can tell me something about a business letter?

Li: Let me try. Generally speaking, a business letter in English consists of eight principal parts.

Wang: What are they?

Li: I think they are "Heading/Letterhead, Date, Inside Name and Address, Salutation, Subject Line, Body of the Letter, Complimentary Close and Signature".

Wang: Wow! Great! You are right. And how to use conventional closings?

Li: Sorry. I'm not sure.

Wang: The conventional closings are often used as follows: "Yours Sincerely, Sincerely Yours, Truly Yours; Yours Faithfully, Yours Respectfully; Very Cordially Yours, Yours Cordially; Best Wishes and Best Regards".

Li: Oh, I see. Is salutation in conformity with Complimentary Closing?

Wang: Of course. Salutation is "Gentlemen", complimentary Closing is "Yours Sincerely"; Salutation is "Dear Sirs", complimentary Closing is "Faithfully Yours".

Li: Today I have learned so much. Thank you, Mrs. Wang.

Wang: I'm very glad you are careful. It's my duty.

 Words and Phrases(单词与短语)

heading /ˈhedɪŋ/   n. 信头
salutation /ˌsæljuˈteɪʃən/   n. 称谓

signature /ˈsɪɡnətʃə/	n. 签名
conventional /kənˈvenʃnl/	adj. 常规的
sincerely /sinˈsiəli/	adj. 真诚的
faithfully /ˈfeiθfəli/	adj. 忠实的
respectfully /riˈspektfəli/	adv. 恭敬地
cordially /ˈkɔːdjəli/	adv. 诚挚地
regards /riˈɡɑːdz/	n. 问候
complimentary closing /ˌkɔmpliˈmentri; ˈkləuziŋ/	结尾客套语
Inside Name and Address	封内地址
Subject Line	标题
Body of the Letter	正文

 ## Notes（注释）

The conventional closings are often used as follows: "Yours Sincerely, Sincerely Yours, Truly Yours（级别相同的个人、公司或部门之间常用）; Yours Faithfully, Yours Respectfully（下级给上级、晚辈给长辈、子公司给总公司常用）; Very Cordially Yours, Yours Cordially（上级给下级、长辈给晚辈、总公司给子公司常用）; Best Wishes and Best Regards（在短信、便条、电传或传真中常用）".

Knowing Some Logistics Documents（了解一些物流单证）

1. Bill of Lading(B/L)（提单）

B/L is one of the most important documents in ocean shipping. It is used mainly in international trade. It must be presented at the port of final destination by the importer in order to claim goods. The functions of B/L: a receipt for the goods shipped, evidence of the contract of carriage, document of title for the goods.（样本见附录 E）

2. Air Waybill（空运运单）

An air waybill is a form of B/L used for the air transport. Each air waybill has three originals and at least six copies. The functions of air waybill: an evidence of a transportation contract, but it is not a document of title or a negotiable document; a receipt of the goods to be dispatched and evidence of the contract of carriage between the carrier and the consignor.（样本见附录 E）

3. Insurance Policy（保险单）

An insurance policy is a document confirming insurance of cargo and indicating the types and amount which the insurance covers. This document is usually issued to the party buying

the insurance.(样本见附录 E)

4. Packing List(装箱单)

A packing list is a document prepared by the shipper when the goods are to be shipped, it includes the following information: the invoice number, buyer, consignee, country of origin, vessel or flight details, port or airport of loading and discharge, place of delivery, shipping marks, container number, weight and cubic of goods, etc. Its prime purpose is to give an inventory of the shipped goods which is required by the customs.(样本见附录 E)

5. Commercial Invoice(商业发票)

The commercial invoice is a document offered by the seller to the buyer. The commercial invoice is issued by the exporter. It provides details of a transaction between the importer and the exporter. Its main function: a check on charges and delivery for the importer, determination on the value of goods, assessment of customs duties, preparation for consular documentation, insurance claims and packing purposes.(样本见附录 E)

6. Certificate of Origin(原产地证书)

A certificate of origin is a document issued by a certifying authority such as a chamber of commerce in the exporter's country. It states the country where the goods are made. It is usually required by countries to set the right duties for the importers.(样本见附录 E)

 Words and Phrases（单词与短语）

cargo /ˈkɑːɡəu/	n. 货物
invoice /ˈinvɔis/	n. 发票
carriage /ˈkæridʒ/	n. 运输，运费
destination /ˌdestiˈneiʃən/	n. 目的地
description /diˈskripʃən/	n. 描述，形容
negotiable /niˈɡəuʃiəbəl/	adj. 可流通的，可转让的
dispatch /diˈspætʃ/	n. 派遣，发送
consignor /kənˈsainə/	n. 委托者，发货人，交付人
cubic /ˈkjuːbik/	n. 体积
transaction /trænˈzækʃən/	n. 处理，交易
assessment /əˈsesmənt/	n. 评估，估价
insurance /inˈʃuərəns/	n. 保险，保险业
authority /ɔːˈθɔrəti/	n. 权威，权力机关
duty /ˈdjuːti/	n. 义务，责任，关税
air waybill	空运运单
packing list	装箱单
insurance policy	保险单
certificate of origin	原产地证书
port of loading	装货港

port of destination	目的港
document of title	物权凭证
customs clearance	通关,清关
chamber of commerce	商会

 Notes(注释)

1. It must be presented at the port of final destination by the importer in order to claim goods. 提单是进口商为在目的地港领取货物时提交的单据。

2. evidence of the contract of carriage 运输合约的证据

3. document of title for the goods 货物的物权凭证

4. Each air waybill has three originals and at least six copies. It is an evidence of a transportation contract, but it is not a document of title or a negotiable document. 每份空运运单有三份正本以及至少六份副本。空运运单是运输合约的一个证明,但它不是物权凭证,也不能转让和流通。

5. Determination on the value of goods, assessment of customs duties, preparation for consular documentation, insurance claims and packing purposes. 货物价值评估、关税估价、准备领事文件、保险索赔以及包装目的。

Dialogue Two

Talking About Bill of Lading(谈论提单)

(Li Gang is a new clerk in Mini Logistics Company. He knows little about bills of lading. So he is learning from his workmate, Wu Liao.)

Li: Good afternoon, Wu Liao. Are you busy now?

Wu: No. Can I help you?

Li: Well. I know little about bills of lading, could you explain them to me in detail?

Wu: I'm glad to do so. First, you should know the form, a B/L may contain these elements: the name of the shipping company(the carrier), the name of the shipper who is usually the exporter or its agent, the name of the consignee, the notify party, the name of the carrying vessel and the voyage No., two ports (port of shipment and port of destination), total packages, freight and charges (freight prepaid or freight to collect), number of original B/L, the signature of the carrier, and B/L issuing place and date.

Li: Oh, I see. Thanks. Then how many types of marine B/L are there in logistics?

Wu: Fifteen.

Li: So much to learn? Could you tell me what they are?

Wu: Of course. They are shipped B/L, received for shipment B/L, clean B/L, unclean B/L, straight B/L, order B/L, open B/L, direct B/L, transshipment B/L, through B/L, combined transport B/L, long form B/L, short form B/L, liner B/L and chartered B/L.

Li: Thanks for giving me such clear explanations.

Wu: It's my pleasure.

Words and Phrases（单词与短语）

category /ˈkætəgəri/	n. 种类
standard /ˈstændəd/	n. 标准
marine /məˈriːn/	adj. 海运的
shipper /ˈʃipə/	n. 托运人
agent /ˈeidʒənt/	n. 代理人
consignee /ˌkɔnsaiˈniː/	n. 收货人
vessel /ˈvesəl/	n. 船
signature /ˈsignitʃə/	n. 签名
carrier /ˈkæriə/	n. 承运人
bill of lading(B/L)	提单
the shipping company	船运公司
the notify party	被通知方
the voyage No.	航次
freight and charges	运费和费用
original B/L	正本提单
B/L issuing place and date	签发提单的地点和时间

Notes（注释）

They are shipped B/L, received for shipment B/L, clean B/L, unclean B/L, straight B/L, order B/L, open B/L, direct B/L, transshipment B/L, through B/L, combined transport B/L, long form B/L, short form B/L, liner B/L and chartered B/L. 它们是已装船提单、备船提单、清洁提单、不清洁提单、记名提单、指示提单、不记名提单、直达提单、转船提单、联运提单、多式联运提单、全式提单、简式提单、班轮提单、租船提单。

Knowledge accumulation（知识积累）

1. One of the most important documents in maritime trade is the bill of lading. 海上贸易最重要的单证之一就是提单。

2. A cargo manifest provides information regarding the cargoes on board. 货物清单提供装上船的货物信息。

3. The shipping note is a commitment to ship the goods from the shipper, and it is the basis to prepare the bill of lading. 托运单是托运人托运货物的承诺，也是填制提单的依据。

4. A mate's receipt is the receipt issued by the carrier when the goods are received on board. 大副收据是承运人收到货物并装船的收据。

5. All of the original Bs/L are negotiable. 所有的正本提单都是可转让的。

 Exercises（练习）

1. Translate the following phrases/sentences into Chinese/English（英汉互译）.

1) conventional closings　　　　　＿＿＿＿＿＿＿＿＿＿＿＿＿＿＿＿

2) document of title for the goods　＿＿＿＿＿＿＿＿＿＿＿＿＿＿＿＿

3) transshipment B/L　　　　　　＿＿＿＿＿＿＿＿＿＿＿＿＿＿＿＿

4) 托运人　　　　　　　　　　　＿＿＿＿＿＿＿＿＿＿＿＿＿＿＿＿

5) 收货人　　　　　　　　　　　＿＿＿＿＿＿＿＿＿＿＿＿＿＿＿＿

6) 发货人　　　　　　　　　　　＿＿＿＿＿＿＿＿＿＿＿＿＿＿＿＿

7) Thank for giving me such clear explanations.

＿＿＿＿＿＿＿＿＿＿＿＿＿＿＿＿＿＿＿＿＿＿＿＿＿＿＿＿＿＿＿＿＿＿＿＿＿＿＿

8) B/L is the receipt of lading from carrier.

＿＿＿＿＿＿＿＿＿＿＿＿＿＿＿＿＿＿＿＿＿＿＿＿＿＿＿＿＿＿＿＿＿＿＿＿＿＿＿

9) 保险单对购买者很重要。

＿＿＿＿＿＿＿＿＿＿＿＿＿＿＿＿＿＿＿＿＿＿＿＿＿＿＿＿＿＿＿＿＿＿＿＿＿＿＿

10) 我已经了解到许多有关单证知识。

＿＿＿＿＿＿＿＿＿＿＿＿＿＿＿＿＿＿＿＿＿＿＿＿＿＿＿＿＿＿＿＿＿＿＿＿＿＿＿

2. Answer the following questions in English（回答问题）.

1) What does "straight B/L" mean?

＿＿＿＿＿＿＿＿＿＿＿＿＿＿＿＿＿＿＿＿＿＿＿＿＿＿＿＿＿＿＿＿＿＿＿＿＿＿＿

2) How many functions do the bills of lading have?

＿＿＿＿＿＿＿＿＿＿＿＿＿＿＿＿＿＿＿＿＿＿＿＿＿＿＿＿＿＿＿＿＿＿＿＿＿＿＿

3) What is the purpose of packing list?

＿＿＿＿＿＿＿＿＿＿＿＿＿＿＿＿＿＿＿＿＿＿＿＿＿＿＿＿＿＿＿＿＿＿＿＿＿＿＿

4) Is an air waybill a form of B/L used for the air transport of goods?

＿＿＿＿＿＿＿＿＿＿＿＿＿＿＿＿＿＿＿＿＿＿＿＿＿＿＿＿＿＿＿＿＿＿＿＿＿＿＿

3. Choose the best answers according to description（选择题）.

(　　)1) A certificate of origin is a ＿＿＿＿ issued by a certifying authority.
　　　　A. document　　B. bill　　　　C. order　　　　D. invoice

(　　)2) The shipping company will tell you when your ＿＿＿＿ is loaded on board.
　　　　A. company　　B. cargo　　　C. document　　D. ship

(　　)3) Logistics documents contain three kinds of documents: government documents, ＿＿＿＿ documents and transport documents.

　　　　　　A. B/L　　　　　　B. insurance　　　C. commercial　　D. packaging

(　)4) Must B/L be presented at the port of final destination by the importer?

　　　　　　A. I don't know.　B. I think so.　　C. No.　　　　　D. Yes.

(　)5) _____ is used in the letters for "上级给下级、长辈给晚辈、总公司给支公司".

　　　　　　A. Truly Yours　　　　　　　　　　B. Yours Faithfully
　　　　　　C. Yours Cordially　　　　　　　　D. Best Wishes

(　)6) Air waybill is not a _____ document.

　　　　　　A. negotiable　　B. contract　　　　C. carriage　　　D. transport

(　)7) Does the bill of lading perform a number of functions? _____.

　　　　　　A. No　　　　　　　　　　　　　　B. Yes
　　　　　　C. No, I don't think so　　　　　　D. Yes, it is

(　)8) The commercial invoice is issued by the _____.

　　　　　　A. carriers　　　B. importers　　　C. exporters　　　D. shippers

(　)9) An insurance policy is a document confirming _____ of cargo.

　　　　　　A. weight　　　　B. number　　　　C. size　　　　　D. insurance

(　)10) What does chartered B/L mean?

　　　　　　A. 全式提单　　　B. 简式提单　　　C. 班轮提单　　　D. 租船提单

4. Reading letter(阅读信件).

Scenario：你方代理20t大豆业务，在收到信用证后，你方将货物装船。请写一封信通知买方，货船将于2005年3月20日由广州港驶往纽约，预计2005年4月30日前到达。为方便对方提货，随函附上相关票据。

Specimen Letter(样信)

Shipping Advice(装船通知)

Dear Mr. Rut,

Re：Your Order No. 3884

　　We are acknowledged with thanks the receipt of your L/C(Letter of Credit) No. G-103. Now we are pleased to advise you that the 20 tons of soybeans(大豆) under the captioned order(标题订单项下的) having been shipped on board s. s. Haiying(海英号) is scheduled to(预计) sail from Guangzhou on March 20 and arrive at New York around April 30(预计将于……左右到达纽约).

　　To facilitate(便于) your carrying of the goods(提货), we are enclosing(附上) copies of the following shipping documents(运输单据), each in duplicate(一式两份)：

　　Invoice No. GW-235

　　Packing List No. GW-264

　　Certificate of Origin No. 539

　　Non-negotiable Bill of Lading(提单副本)No. EKH-103

> Insurance Policy No. 2948
>
> Survey Report No. FR 293
>
> We hope this shipment will reach you in perfect condition and look forward to your further orders.

根据信件内容选择问题最合适的答语。

(　　)1) Tom: Who is this letter written to?

　　　　Jane: _____.

　　　　A. Mr. Scenario　　　　　　　　B. Mr. Rut

　　　　C. Dadou　　　　　　　　　　　D. Insurance Company

(　　)2) Tom: What kind of letter is this?

　　　　Jane: It is _____.

　　　　A. shipping advice　　　　　　　B. unloading advice

　　　　C. port advice　　　　　　　　　D. invitation

(　　)3) Tom: How many copies do shipping documents have to facilitate carrying of the goods?

　　　　Jane: _____.

　　　　A. Only one　　　　　　　　　　B. Three

　　　　C. In duplicate　　　　　　　　　D. In triplicate(一式三份)

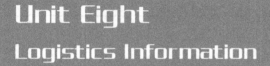

Unit Eight
Logistics Information

Part One Learning Target (学习目标)

1. To know the role of logistics information.
2. To understand information technology in logistics.
3. To learn the functions of logistics information systems.
4. To develop communication skill in introducing information.

Part Two Learning Contents (学习内容)

Text One

Information Technology(信息技术)

1. The Importance of Information(信息的重要性)

Information is the key to the success of a supply chain, because it enables management to make decisions over a broad scope that crosses both functions and companies. Information deeply affects every part of the supply chain in many ways. Information is a driver whose importance has grown as companies become more and more efficient and responsive. Information is the most valuable in reducing costs and improving responsiveness in a supply chain.

2. The Features of Information(信息的特点)

Information must be accurate, accessible, timely and of the right kind.

3. Information Work(信息工作)

Nowadays all firms are in a competitive society. Timely and accurate information is important to them. Thus information work is necessary. In general, information work includes information gathering, information service, information technology developing and applying, information system, information education, information policy, information theory method.

4. The Requirement of Information in Logistics(物流中信息需求)

Information is required at every stage and at every level in logistics. It is usually the case that technology reduces costs. That means IT can effectively bring increased profits. There are different levels of information required in logistics. They can be identified as: the strategic levels (medium-term to long-term planning), the tactical levels (medium-term to short-term planning), the operational levels (shorter-term to minute-by-minute decisions).

5. Defining Information Technology(IT)(信息技术定义)

IT refers to the technology which is to gain, transmit, process, regenerate and use information. In general, IT is the technology which can expand man's information processing ability.

IT includes sensor technology, communication technology, computer technology, database technology, control technology and so on.

 Words and Phrases (单词与短语)

accurate /ˈækjərit/	adj. 准确的
accessible /əkˈsesəbəl/	adj. 容易得到的
theory /ˈθiəri/	n. 理论
tactical /ˈtæktikəl/	adj. 策略上的
operational /ˌɔpəˈreiʃənəl/	adj. 运作的
transmit /trænsˈmit/	v. 传递
regenerate /riˈdʒenəreit/	v. 使再生
ability /əˈbiliti/	n. 能力

 Notes (注释)

1. IT refers to the technology which is to gain, transmit, process, regenerate and use information. In general, IT is the technology which can expand man's information processing ability. 信息技术是指获取、传递、处理、再生和利用信息的技术，泛指能拓展人的信息处理能力的技术。

2. IT includes sensor technology, communication technology, computer technology, database technology, control technology and so on. 信息技术包括传感技术、通信技术、计算机技术、数据库技术、控制技术，等等。

Dialogue One

How Important Information Is!（信息多么重要！）

(Mr. Smith have just come back from his business trip to America. He is talking his experiences to his friend, Jack.)

Jack: Hello! Long time no see! Where have you been?

Smith: I have just come back from Omaha. I have received a big order on equipments. I have broadened my horizons, and have a different understanding of things now!

Jack: What is different now?

Smith: Everything goes efficiently. One of my first concerns is information about shipping. You can find every liner service on the North American line, and you can see lots of containers piling at the port, like the sea of containers. Every day many ships come in and go out orderly.

Jack: Then, what is efficient?

Smith: For example, there is one unique service in the tracing system. They have installed a radio frequency identification equipment on the ships and trucks. This enables us to make real time tracing and reporting of the cargo flow.

Jack: Does it mean the customers can get real time information about their cargos? Can I phone to check on the movement of my cargo at any time?

Smith: Of course, but you needn't. The only thing you need to do is to connect your computer to the Internet, find the website of companies and login in with your company name and the password. You just need to enter the number of the container, and then you'll know where your container is.

Jack: Oh, information is really important for every business field.

 Words and Phrases（单词与短语）

concern /kənˈsən/	n. 担心，忧虑
liner /ˈlainə/	n. 油轮，轮船
install /inˈstɔːl/	v. 安装
frequency /ˈfriːkwənsi/	n. 频率
equipment /iˈkwipmənt/	n. 设备
enable /iˈneibl/	v. 使能够
login /ˈlɔːɡin/	n. 注册
broaden /ˈbrɔːdn/	v. 拓展，扩大
horizon /həˈraizən/	n. 眼界
frequency identification equipment	频率辨别设备

tracing system　　　　　　　　　追踪系统
make real time tracing　　　　　实行实时跟踪

 Notes（注释）

The only thing you need to do is to connect your computer to the Internet, find the website of companies and login in with your company name and the password. 你要做的唯一的事就是连接互联网，找到公司的网站，注册你公司的名称和密码。

Text Two

Logistics Information Technology（物流信息技术）

1. Defining Logistics Information Technology (LIT)（物流信息技术定义）

LIT refers to the applications of modern information technology in each logistics operation.

LIT includes: Bar Code, Radio Frequency Identification technology (RFID), Global Positioning System(GPS), Geographic Information System.

2. Defining the Logistics Information System（物流信息系统定义）

The Logistics Information System can be defined as: the system is composed of people, equipment and procedures which can gather, sort, analyze, evaluate information and then provide them accurately for the correspondant decision-makers in time so that they can make qualified logistics decisions.

3. Features of the Logistics Information System（物流信息系统的特征）

Features of the Logistics Information System: openness, extendibility, flexibility, cooperativity, dynamic nature, quick response, integration of information, supporting the processing.

4. Main Components of the Logistics Information System in Enterprises（企业内部物流信息系统的主要组成）

1) Warehouse Management System (WMS)　2) Transportation Management System (TMS)　3) Material Requirements Planning System(MRP)　4) Making Resource Planning System(MRPS)　5) Enterprise Resource Planning System (ERPS)　6) Decision Support System(DSS)　7) Management Information System (MIS)　8) Point of Sells (POS)　9) Electronic Order System (EOS)

5. Components of the Logistics Information System（物流信息系统的主要组成）

1) The order processing system

2) Research and intelligence system

3) Decision support system

4) Reports and outputs system

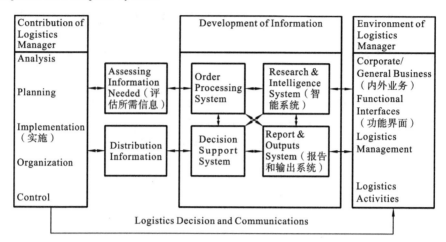

6. ICT Application in International Logistics（信息技术在国际物流中的应用）

With the unceasing expansion of international logistics in the world, logistics operations must develop rapidly. So information communication technology (ICT) and intelligent transportation system (ITS) are especially important in the field of international logistics management. They can be divided into three levels: the application of IT (bar code technology, automatic picking system, automatic access system, automatic billing system); the combination of information and communication technology (global positioning of satellite, Internet); the application of intelligent technology (digital warehouse, automatic groupage system, logistics distribution system of city socialization).

Words and Phrases（单词与短语）

application /ˌæpliˈkeiʃən/	n. 应用
involvement /inˈvɔlvmənt/	n. 参与,加入
appropriate /əˈprəuprieit/	adj. 适当的
intelligence /inˈtelidʒəns/	n. 智力
openness /ˈəupənnəs/	n. 开放性
extendibility /iksˈtendibiliti/	n. 扩展性
flexibility /ˌfleksiˈbiliti/	n. 灵活性
cooperativity /kəuˌɔpərəˈtivəti/	n. 协同性
response /riˈspɔns/	n. 反应
integration /ˌintiˈgreiʃən/	n. 集成
dynamic /daiˈnæmik/	adj. 动态的

Notes（注释）

1. LIT refers to the applications of modern information technology in each logistics

operation. 物流信息技术指的是现代信息技术在物流各作业环节的应用。

2. Bar Code(条形码), Radio Frequency Identification technology(RFID)(无线射频技术), Global Positioning System(GPS)(全球卫星定位系统), Geographic Information System (地理信息系统).

3. the system is composed of people, equipment and procedures which can gather, sort, analyze, evaluate information and then provide them accurately for the correspondant decision-makers in time so that they can make qualified logistics decisions. 由人、设备和程序组成的系统,能够对信息进行分类、分析、评价,并及时准确地提供给相关的决策者,以便他们能作出高质量的物流决策。

4. openness, extendibility, flexibility, cooperativity, dynamic nature, quick response, integration of information, supporting the processing 开放性、可扩展性、灵活性、协同性、动态性、快速反应、信息的集成性,支持远程处理

5. 1) Warehouse Management System(WMS)　仓储管理系统
2) Transportation Management System(TMS)　运输管理系统
3) Material Requirements Planning System(MRP)　物料需求计划系统
4) Making Resource Planning System(MRPS)　制造资源计划系统
5) Enterprise Resource Planning System (ERPS)　企业资源计划系统
6) Decision Support System(DSS)　决策资源系统
7) Management Information System(MIS)　管理信息系统
8) Point of Sells(POS)　销售点信息系统
9) Electronic Order System(EOS)　电子自动订货系统

6. So information communication technology(ICT) and intelligent transportation system (ITS) are especially important in the field of international logistics management. ICT and ITS can be divided into three levels: the application of IT(bar code technology, automatic picking system, automatic access system, automatic billing system); the combination of information and communication technology (global positioning of satellite, Internet); the application of intelligent technology (digital warehouse, automatic groupage system, logistics distribution system of city socialization). 因此,在国际物流管理领域中信息与通讯技术和智能交通系统显得尤为重要。ICT 和 ITS 可以分成三个层面:信息技术的应用(条码技术、自动分拣系统、自动存取系统、自动收费系统);信息与通讯技术的结合(全球卫星定位系统、因特网);智能化技术的应用(数据仓库、自动配货系统、城市社会化的物流配送系统)。

Dialogue Two

What Magical Scanners!（多么神奇的扫描仪呀!）

(Li Yi, a student majoring in logistics, is talking about the scanners with James, a *student majoring in computer.*)

James: Hello! Welcome.

Li: Thanks. Excuse me, how long have you been in this college?

James: One year. What can I do for you?

Li: I wonder what the salespersons in the shop use to calculate the price of the goods. Could you introduce it to me?

James: No problem. They use auto identification (ID) systems such as bar coding and electronic scanning.

Li: Bar coding and electronic scanning? What is it?

James: That's easy. It's a scanner. The scanner can distinguish and exchange information on the price tag. With the development of information technology, different kinds of scanners are widely used in many fields. For example, a typical application is to track receipts at warehouses and retail sales. Now the use of the scanners can speed up the operation of management. The quality of our life is also greatly improved.

Li: You are right. Thanks to the development of information technology, a small equipment can help us so much. Thanks for your introducing.

James: It's my pleasure.

Hand-held laser scanner (手持激光扫描仪)

HP 7000n Scanner (惠普 7000n 扫描仪)

Bar code scanner (条码扫描仪)

 Words and Phrases (单词与短语)

scanner /ˈskænə/   n. 扫描仪
laser /ˈleizə/   n. 激光
typical /ˈtipikəl/   adj. 有代表性的,典型的

application /ˌæpliˈkeiʃən/	n. 应用
the price tag	价格标签
speed up	(使)加速

Notes（注释）

With the development of information technology, different kinds of scanners are widely used in many fields. 随着信息技术的发展,不同种类的扫描仪能广泛应用于许多领域。

Knowledge accumulation（知识积累）

1. Supply chain management means to design, plan and control the information flow, material flow and cash flow in order to strengthen the competitiveness. 供应链管理就是对信息流、物料流和资金流进行设计、计划和控制以增强竞争力。(或:供应链管理是指为增强竞争力而对信息流、物料流和资金流进行的设计、策划和控制。)

2. Information is a key to the success of logistics. 信息是物流成功的关键。

3. Information is crucial to the performance of a supply chain. 信息对供应链的运作是至关重要的。

4. Information flow was brought into full use in each link of the logistics activities. 信息流在物流活动中的各个环节上发挥了应有的作用。

5. IT provides the underlying links as well as the data collection and analysis platform for these companies to deliver goods purchased online. 信息技术提供了潜在的联系,还为这些传递在线出售商品的公司提供了数据收集和分析的平台。

6. Information is of vital importance for supply chain managers as it supplies useful facts to them. 信息对供应链经理们很重要,因为它向他们提供实用的事实。

7. Managers must understand how information is gathered and analyzed. 经理们必须明白信息是怎样收集和分析的。

8. An information system generally consists of hardware and software. 信息系统通常包括硬件和软件。

9. As a fact, timely and accurate information has value. 事实上,及时、准确的信息意味着价值。

Exercises（练习）

1. Translate the following phrases/sentences into Chinese/English（英汉互译）.

1) 信息技术　　　　　　　　　＿＿＿＿＿＿＿＿＿＿＿＿＿＿＿＿＿＿＿

2) 运输管理系统　　　　　　　＿＿＿＿＿＿＿＿＿＿＿＿＿＿＿＿＿＿＿

3) 数据库　　　　　　　　　　＿＿＿＿＿＿＿＿＿＿＿＿＿＿＿＿＿＿＿

4) Bar Code　　　　　　　　＿＿＿＿＿＿＿＿＿＿＿＿＿＿＿＿＿＿＿

5) control technology　　　＿＿＿＿＿＿＿＿＿＿＿＿＿＿＿＿＿＿＿

6) information processing　＿＿＿＿＿＿＿＿＿＿＿＿＿＿＿＿＿＿＿

7) The information at tactical levels are mainly used to make medium-term to short-term plan such as forecasting, scheduling and resource planning.

＿＿＿＿＿＿＿＿＿＿＿＿＿＿＿＿＿＿＿＿＿＿＿＿＿＿＿＿＿＿＿＿＿＿＿＿＿

8) Lead time will be shortened with the help of IT.

＿＿＿＿＿＿＿＿＿＿＿＿＿＿＿＿＿＿＿＿＿＿＿＿＿＿＿＿＿＿＿＿＿＿＿＿＿

9) 在日常生活中，信息技术帮助我们大大地提高了我们的生活质量。

＿＿＿＿＿＿＿＿＿＿＿＿＿＿＿＿＿＿＿＿＿＿＿＿＿＿＿＿＿＿＿＿＿＿＿＿＿

10) 信息技术的发展真正地使我们感到更快捷、更方便、更安全。

＿＿＿＿＿＿＿＿＿＿＿＿＿＿＿＿＿＿＿＿＿＿＿＿＿＿＿＿＿＿＿＿＿＿＿＿＿

2. Answer the following questions in English(回答问题).

1) Do you enjoy information technology in your daily life?

＿＿＿＿＿＿＿＿＿＿＿＿＿＿＿＿＿＿＿＿＿＿＿＿＿＿＿＿＿＿＿＿＿＿＿＿＿

2) What does logistics information system include?

＿＿＿＿＿＿＿＿＿＿＿＿＿＿＿＿＿＿＿＿＿＿＿＿＿＿＿＿＿＿＿＿＿＿＿＿＿

3) What are the features of information?

＿＿＿＿＿＿＿＿＿＿＿＿＿＿＿＿＿＿＿＿＿＿＿＿＿＿＿＿＿＿＿＿＿＿＿＿＿

4) How many features does the logistics information system have in the text?

＿＿＿＿＿＿＿＿＿＿＿＿＿＿＿＿＿＿＿＿＿＿＿＿＿＿＿＿＿＿＿＿＿＿＿＿＿

3. Choose the best answers according to description(选择题).

(　　)1) What have they installed on the ships and trucks in Dialogue One? ＿＿＿＿＿＿.
　　　A. Camera　　　　　B. Vidicon(摄像机)
　　　C. Scanner　　　　　D. A radio frequency identification equipment

(　　)2) What is ▮▮▮▮▮▮▮ ?
　　　A. A scanner.　　B. An eraser.　　C. Bar code.　　D. A ruler.

(　　)3) Transportation management also needs ＿＿＿＿＿＿ System.
　　　A. GP　　　　　　　　　　　B. Geographic Information
　　　C. IT　　　　　　　　　　　D. All above

(　　)4) A scanner can help us ＿＿＿＿＿＿ information.
　　　A. collect　　　　　　　　　B. distinguish
　　　C. exchange　　　　　　　　D. All above

(　　)5) Which one is not the feature of Logistics ITS? ＿＿＿＿＿＿.
　　　A. Openness　　　　　　　　B. Cooperativity
　　　C. Expensiveness　　　　　　D. Quick response

(　　)6) Timely and ＿＿＿＿＿＿ information is more critical(关键的).

A. slow B. new C. accurate D. good

( )7) Which one is not the level of information required in logistics?
A. the strategic levels B. the operational levels
C. the tactical levels D. packaging

( )8) What does ICT mean?
A. 信息与通信 B. 电子数据转换
C. 信息与通讯技术 D. 智能交通系统

( )9) Which one is not included in the application of IT? _____.
A. bar code technology B. artificially charge(人工收费)
C. automatic picking system D. automatic billing system

( )10) How can we know where our container is?
The only thing is to _____
① find the website of companies and login in with your company name and the password ② enter the number of the container ③ connect your computer to the Internet. 给以上三个答案排序。
A. ①②③ B. ②③① C. ③①② D. ③②①

4. Reading passage(阅读小短文).

Logistics Information

Supply chain managers use information to make many important decisions. Setting inventory levels requires downstream information from customers on demand, upstream information from suppliers on availability, and also the information on current inventory levels, costs, and margins. Determining transportation policies requires information on customers, suppliers, routes, costs, times, and quantities to be shipped. Deciding facilities quantities requires information on demand and suppliers, as well as information on capacities, revenues, and costs within the company.

根据短文内容选择问题最合适的答语。

( )1) What do supply chain managers use to make many important decisions?
A. International trade. B. Logistics.
C. Government regulations. D. Logistics information.

( )2) What decision requires information on demand and suppliers, as well as information on capacities, revenues, and costs within the company?
A. Setting inventory levels.
B. Decisions on facilities.
C. Determining transportation policies.
D. None.

( )3) What kind of information is required to determine transportation policies?
A. Information on customers. B. Information on suppliers.
C. Information on routes. D. All above.

附录 A 物流专业词汇

article reserves /ˈɑːtikl,riˈzəːvz/ 物品储存量
assembly /əˈsembli/ 组配
automatic guided vehicle (AGV) /ˌɔːtəˈmætik,ˈgaidid,ˈviːikl/ 自动导引车
automatic warehouse /ˈwɛəhaus/ 自动化仓库
bar code /bɑː,kəud/ 条码
bonded warehouse /ˈbɔndid/ 保税仓库
box car /bɔks,kɑː/ 箱式车
cargo under customs' supervision /ˈkɑːgəu,ˈʌndə,ˈkʌstəməz,ˌsjuːpəˈviʒən/ 海关监管货物
chill space /tʃil,speis/ 冷藏区
cold chain /kəuld,tʃein/ 冷链
combined transport /kəmˈbaind,trænsˈpɔːt/ 联合运输
commodity inspection /kəˈmɔditi,inˈspekʃən/ 进出口商品检验
Continuous Replenishment Program (CRP) /kənˈtinjuəs,riˈpleniʃmənt,ˈprəugræm/ 连续库存补充计划
containerization /kənˌteinərai'zeiʃən/ 集装化
containerized transport /kənˈteinəraizd/ 集装运输
container terminal /ˈtəːminəl/ 集装箱码头
conveyor /kənˈveiə/ 输送机
cross docking /krɔs,ˈdɔkiŋ/ 直接换装
customized logistics /ˈkʌstəmaizd,ləuˈdʒistiks/ 定制物流
customs broker /ˈkʌstəmz,ˈbrəukə/ 报关行
customs declaration /ˌdekləˈreiʃən/ 报关单
cycle stock /ˈsaikl,stɔk/ 经常库存
distribution center /distriˈbjuːʃən,ˈsentə/ 配送中心
distribution logistics /distriˈbjuːʃən,ləˈdʒistiks/ 销售物流
distribution processing /prəuˈsesiŋ/ 流通加工
Distribution Requirements Planning (DRP) /riˈkwaiəmənts,ˈplæniŋ/ 配送需要计划
Distribution Resource Planning (DRP II) /riˈsɔːs/ 配送资源计划

door-to-door /ˈdɔːtəˈdɔː/ 门到门
drop and pull transport /drɔp,pul/ 甩挂运输
Economic Order Quantity（EOQ）/ˌiːkəˈnɔmik,ˈkwɔntiti/ 经济订货量
Efficient Customer Response(ECR) /iˈfiʃənt,riˈspɔns/ 有效客户反映
Electronic Order System（EOS）/ilekˈtrɔnik,ˈsistəm/ 电子订货系统
Enterprise Resource Planning（ERP）/ˈentəpraiz/ 企业资源计划
environmental logistics /enˌvaiərənˈmentl/ 绿色物流
export supervised warehouse /eksˈpɔːt,ˈsjuːpəvaizd/ 出口监管仓库
external logistics /eksˈtəːnl/ 社会物流
Fixed Quantity System（FQS）/fikst,ˈkwɔntiti/ 定量订货方式
Fixed Interval System（FIS）/ˈintəvəl/ 定期订货方式
fork lift truck /fɔːk,lift,trʌk/ 叉车
freeze space /friːz,speis/ 冷冻区
full container load（FCL）/ful,ləud/ 整箱货
full container ship 全集装箱船
goods collection /gudz,kəˈlekʃn/ 集货
goods shed /ʃed/ 料棚
goods shelf /ʃelf/ 货架
goods stack /stæk/ 货垛
goods yard /jɑːd/ 货场
handing carrying /ˈhændiŋ,ˈkæriiŋ/ 搬运
humidity controlled space /hjuːˈmiditi,kənˈtrəuld/ 控湿储存区
in bulk /in,bʌlk/ 散装化
inland container depot /ˈinlənd,ˈdepəu/ 公路集装箱中转站
inspection /inˈspekʃən/ 检验
intangible loss /inˈtændʒəbəl,lɔs/ 无形消耗
internal logistics /inˈtəːnəl/ 企业物流
international freight forwarding agent /ˌintəˈnæʃənəl,freit,ˈfɔːwədiŋ,ˈeidʒənt/ 国际货运代理
international logistics 国际物流
international multimodal transport /ˌmʌltiˈməudəl/ 国际多式联运
international transportation cargo insurance /ˌtrænspɔːˈteiʃən,inˈʃuərəns/ 国际货物运输保险
international through railway transport /θruː,ˈreilwei/ 国际铁路联运
inventory control /ˈinvəntri/ 库存控制
inventory cycle time /taim/ 库存周期
joint distribution /dʒɔint/ 共同配送
Just -in -time（JIT）准时制
just-in-time logistics 准时制物流
land bridge transport /lænd,bridʒ/ 大陆桥运输
lead time /liːd/ 前置期（或提前期）

less than container load (LCL) /les,ðæn/ 拼箱货
liner transport /ˈlainə/ 班轮运输
loading and unloading /ˈləudiŋ,ʌnˈləudiŋ/ 装卸
logistics activity /ækˈtiviti/ 物流活动
logistics alliance /əˈlaiəns/ 物流联盟
logistics center 物流中心
logistics cost /kɔst/ 物流成本
logistics cost control 物流成本管理
logistics documents /ˈdɔkjumənts/ 物流单证
logistics enterprise 物流企业
logistics information /ˌinfəˈmeiʃən/ 物流信息
logistics management /ˈmænidʒmənt/ 物流管理
logistics modulus /ˈmɔdjuləs/ 物流模数
logistics network /ˈnetwəːk/ 物流网络
logistics operation /ˌɔpəˈreiʃən/ 物流作业
Logistics Resource Planning (LRP) 物流资源计划
logistics strategy management /ˈstrætidʒi/ 物流战略管理
logistics technology /tekˈnɔlədʒi/ 物流技术
Manufacturing Resource Planning (MRP II) /ˌmænjuˈfæktʃəriŋ/ 制造资源计划
Material Requirements Planning (MRP) /məˈtiəriəl/ 物料需要计划
military logistics /ˈmilitəri/ 军事物流
neutral packaging /ˈnjuːtrəl,ˈpækidʒiŋ/ 中性包装
order cycle time /ˈɔːdə/ 订货处理周期
order picking /ˈpikiŋ/ 拣选
outsourcing /ˈautˌsɔːsiŋ/ 业务外包
package /ˈpækidʒ/ 包装
packaging of nominated brand /ˈpækidʒiŋ,ɔv,ˈnɔmineitid,brænd/ 定牌包装
pallet /ˈpælit/ 托盘
palletizing /ˈpæliˌtaiziŋ/ 托盘包装
production logistics /prəˈdʌkʃən/ 生产物流
Quick Response (QR) /kwik/ 快速反映
railway container yard /ˈreilwei/ 铁路集装箱场
receiving space /riˈsiːviŋ/ 收货区
returned logistics /riˈtəːnd/ 回收物流
safety stock /ˈseiftiˌstɔk/ 安全库存
sales package /ˈseilz/ 销售包装
shipping agency /ˈʃipiŋ,ˈeidʒənsi/ 船务代理
shipping by chartering /baiˌˈtʃɑːtəriŋ/ 租船运输
shipping space 发货区

sorting /ˈsɔːtiŋ/ 分拣
specific cargo container /spiˈsifik/ 特种货物集装箱
stacking /ˈstækiŋ/ 堆码
stereoscopic warehouse /steriəˈskɔpik/ 立体仓库
storage /ˈstɔːridʒ/ 保管
storehouse /ˈstɔːˌhaus/ 库房
storing /ˈstɔːriŋ/ 储存
Supply Chain Management (SCM) /səˈplai ˌtʃein/ 供应链管理
tally /ˈtæli/ 理货
third-party logistics (TPL) /θəːd-pɑːti/ 第三方物流
tangible loss /ˈtændʒəbl ˌlɔs/ 有形消耗
temperature controlled space /ˈtempəritʃə ˌkənˈtrəuld/ 温度可控区
through transport /θruː/ 直达运输
transfer transport /trænsˈfəː/ 中转运输
transportation /ˌtrænspɔːˈteiʃən/ 运输
transport package 运输包装
Twenty-foot Equivalent Unit (TEU) /ˈtwentifut ˌiˈkwivələnt ˌˈjuːnit/ 20英尺标准箱
value-added logistics service /ˈvæljuːˈædid ˌˈsəːvis/ 增值物流服务
unit loading and unloading 单元装卸
Vendor Manage Inventory (VMI) /ˈvendə ˌˈmænidʒ/ 供应商管理库存
virtual logistics /ˈvəːtjuəl/ 虚拟物流
virtual warehouse /ˈvəːtjuəl/ 虚拟仓库
warehouse layout /ˈleiaut/ 仓库布局
warehouse management 仓库管理
waste material logistics /weist/ 废弃物物流
zero-inventory logistics /ˈziərəu/ 零库存技术

附录 B　其他常见物流术语　＞＞＞

一、其他物流术语（按汉语表达意思分类）

1. ……表

delivery schedule /diˈlivəri ˈʃedjuːəl/ 交货计划表
financial statement of account /faiˈnænʃəl ˈsteitmənt əˈkaunt/ 账户财务报表
statistical document of export /stəˈtistikəl/ 出口统计报表
statistical document of import /ˈimpɔːt/ 进口统计报表
statement of account message /ˈsteitmənt ˈmesidʒ/ 账户报表报文

2. ……报告

first sample test report /fəːst ˈsɑːmpl test riˈpɔːt/ 首样测试报告
process data report /ˈdeitə/ 工艺数据报告
product performance report /ˈprɔdʌkt pəˈfɔːməns/ 产品性能报告
product specification report /ˌspesifiˈkeiʃən/ 产品规格型号报告
test report 测试报告

3. ……报关单

cargo declaration (arrival) /ˌdekəˈreiʃən əˈraivəl/ 到港货物报关单
cargo declaration (departure) /diˈpɑːtʃə/ 离港货物报关单
customs declaration (post parcels) /pəust ˈpɑːsəl/ 邮包报关单
customs declaration with commercial and item detail /wið kəˈməːʃəl ˈaitəm ˈdiːteil/ 有商业和项目细节的报关单
customs declaration without commercial detail 无商业细节的报关单
customs declaration without item detail 无项目细节的报关单
customs immediate release declaration /iˈmiːdiət riˈliːs/ 海关即刻放行报关单
EC carnet /ˌjuərəˈpiːən kəˈmjuːniti ˈkɑːnei/ 欧共体海关转运报关单
goods declaration for customs transit /ˈtrænsit/ 海关转运货物报关单
goods declaration for exportation /ˌekspɔːˈteiʃən/ 出口货物报关单
goods declaration for home use /həum juːz/ 内销货物报关单
goods declaration for importation /ˌimpɔːˈteiʃən/ 进口货物报关单

TIR carnet　　TIR 国际公路运输报关单
TIF form /fɔːm/ TIF 国际铁路运输报关单

4. ……单

charges note /ˈtʃɑːdʒiz/ 铁路费用单
collection order /kəˈlekʃən/ 托收单
commission note /kəˈmiʃən/ 佣金单
consignment order /kənˈsainmənt/ 寄售单
cover note /ˈkʌvə/ 承保单
credit note /ˈkredit/ 贷记单
debit note /ˈdebit/ 借记单
delivery order /diˈlivəri/ 提货单
despatch note (post parcels) /disˈpætʃ, ˈpɑːsəlz/ 邮递包裹投递单
documentary credit amendment /əˈmendmənt/ 跟单信用证更改单
documentary credit letter of indemnity /inˈdemnitiː/ 跟单信用证赔偿单
documents presentation form /ˌprezənˈteiʃən/ 单证提交单
enquiry /inˈkwaiəri/ 询价单
exchange control declaration, export /iksˈtʃeindʒ/ 出口结汇核销单
factored credit note /ˈfæktəd/ 代理贷记单
handling order 装卸单
hire order /ˈhaiə/ 租用单
insurance policy /ˈpɔləsi/ 保险单
internal transport order 内部运输单
invoicing data sheet /ˈinvɔisiŋ, ʃiːt/ 产品售价单
lease order /liːs/ 租赁单
packing list 装箱单
port charges documents /pɔːt, ˈtʃɑːdʒiz/ 港口费用单
purchase order /ˈpəːtʃəs/ 订购单
repair order /riˈpɛə/ 修理单
re-sending consignment note /riːˈsendiŋ/ 铁路运输退运单
road list 陆运单
stores requisition /ˌrekwiˈziʃən/ 领料单
swap order /swɔp/ 换货单
tax demand /diˈmɑːnd/ 催税单
weight list /weit/ 重量单
warehouse warrant /ˈwɔrənt/ 入库单

5. ……单证/许可证/证

combined transport document (generic) /dʒəˈnerik/ 联运单证（通用）
control document T5 T5 管理单证（退运单证）（欧共体用）
despatch note model T1 /ˈmɔdəl/ T1 出口单证（内部转运报关单）（欧共体用）

despatch note model T2 T2出口单证(原产地证明书)

despatch note model T2L T2L出口单证(原产地证明书)(欧共体用)

despatch note model T T出口单证(海关转运报关单)(欧共体用)

multimodal/combined transport document (generic) /ˌmʌltiˈməudəl/ 多式联运单证(通用)

non-negotiable maritime transport document (generic) /ˈnɔniˈɡəuʃjəbl, ˈmæritaim/ 不可转让的海运单证(通用)

recharging document /riːˈtʃɑːdʒiŋ/ 分段计费单证

related document /riˈleitid/ 有关单证

single administrative document /ˈsiŋɡl, ædˈminiˌstreitiv/ 欧共体统一单证

statistical and other administrative internal documents /stəˈtistikəl/ 统计及其他管理用内部单证

universal (multipurpose) transport document /juːniˈvəːsəl, mʌltiˈpəːpəs/ 通用(多用)运输单证

embargo permit /emˈbɑːɡəu, pəˈmit/ 禁运货物许可证

export licence /ˈlaisəns/ 出口许可证

foreign exchange permit /ˈfɔrin/ 调汇许可

import licence 进口许可证

documentary credit 跟单信用证

insurance certificate /səˈtifikit/ 保险凭证

gate pass /ɡeitˌpɑːs/ 通行证

6. ……订单/付款单

blanket order /ˈblæŋkit/ 总订单

call off order /ˈkɔːlɔf/ 分订单

rush order /rʌʃ/ 紧急订单

sample order /ˈsɑːmpl/ 样品订单

sport order /spɔːt/ 现货订单

spare parts order /spɛəˌpɑːts/ 备件订单

extended payment order /iksˈtendid/ 扩展付款单

multiple payment order /ˈmʌltipl/ 多重付款单

7. ……估价单/数量单

direct payment valuation /diˈrekt, ˈpeimənt, ˌvæljuːˈeiʃən/ 直接支付估价单

quantity valuation request /ˌvæljuːˈeiʃən, riˈkwest/ 数量估价单

provisional payment valuation /prəˈviʒənəl/ 临时支付估价单

contract BOQ (Bill of Quantieies) /kənˈtrækt/ 合同数量单

priced tender BOQ /praistˌtendə/ 标价投标数量单

unpriced tender BOQ /ʌnˈpraist/ 不察价投标数量单

8. ……合同/确认

contract /kənˈtrækt/ 合同

government contract /ˈɡʌvənmənt/ 政府合同

acknowledgement of order /əkˈnɔlidʒmənt/ 订单确认
booking confirmation /ˈbukiŋ, ˌkɔnfəˈmeiʃən/ 订舱确认
escort official recognition /ˈeskɔːt, əˈfiʃəl, ˌrekəgˈniʃən/ 押运正式确认

9. ……回复

document response (Customs) /riˈspɔns/ 海关公文回复
error response (Customs) /ˈerə/ 海关误差回复
general response (Customs) /ˈdʒenərəl/ 海关一般回复
package response (Customs) 海关一揽子回复
purchase order response 订购单回复
response to query /ˈkwiəri/ 查询回复
tax calculation /confirmation response (Customs) /ˌkælkjəˈleiʃən, ˌkɔnfəˈmeiʃən/ 海关计税/确认回复

10. ……汇票/发票

banker's draft /drɑːft/ 银行汇票
bill of exchange 汇票
consignment invoice /kənˈsainmənt, ˈinˌvɔis/ 寄售发票
consolidated invoice /kənˈsɔlideitid/ 合并发票
commercial invoice /kəˈməːʃəl/ 商业发票
corrected invoice /kəˈrektid/ 更正发票
consul invoice /ˈkɔnsəl/ 领事发票
customs invoice 海关发票
delcredere invoice /delˈkreidəriː/ 保兑发票
factored invoice /ˈfæktəd/ 代理发票
forwarder's invoice 货运代理发票
freight invoice /freit/ 运费发票
hire invoice /ˈhaiə/ 租用发票
insurer's invoice /inˈʃuərəz/ 保险人发票
lease invoice /liːs/ 租赁发票
proforma invoice /prəˈfɔːmə/ 形式发票
partial invoice /ˈpɑːʃəl/ 部分发票
prepayment invoice /ˈpriːpeimənt/ 预付发票
self-billed invoice /ˈselfbild/ 自用发票
tax invoice 税务发票

11. ……清单

value declaration 货物价值申报清单
bordereau /ˌbɔːdəˈrəu/ 公路运输货物清单
cargo manifest /ˈmænifest/ 载货清单
container manifest (unit packing list) 集装箱载货清单
freight manifest 载货运费清单

12. ……请求/书

purchase order change request /ri'kwest/ 订购单变更请求
request for delivery instructions /in'strʌkʃənz/ 交货说明请求
civil liability for oil certificate /'sivl, ˌlaiə'biliti/ 油污民事责任书
letter of intent /'letə, in'tent/ 意向书
shipper's letter of instructions(air) 托运人说明书(空运)
end use authorization /ˌɔ:θəri'zeiʃən/ 最终使用授权书

13. ……申报单/申报

dangerous goods declaration /'deindʒərəs/ 危险货物申报单
insurance declaration sheet (bordereau) /ˌbɔ:də'rəu/ 保险申报单(明细表)
intrastate declaration /ˌintrə'steit/ 国际贸易统计申报单
ship's stores declaration /ʃips, stɔ:z/ 船用物品申报单
tax declaration (value added tax) 增值税申报单
tax declaration (general) 普通税申报单
crew's effects declaration /kru:z, i'fekts/ 出国人员物品申报
exchange control declaration (import) 进口外汇管理申报

14. ……声明/申明/说明

A. TR. 1 movement certificate /'mu:vmənt/ A. TR. 1 移动声明
declaration of origin 原产地申明
delivery instructions 交货说明
forwarding instructions /'fɔ:wədiŋ/ 货运说明
manufacturing instructions /ˌmænju'fæktʃəriŋ/ 制造说明
operating instructions /'ɔpəˌreitiŋ/ 操作说明
packing instructions 包装说明
shipping instructions 装运说明

15. ……申请/申请书/申请表

application for exchange allocation /ˌæpli'keiʃən, ˌælə'keiʃən/ 调汇申请
booking request /'bukiŋ, ri'kwest/ 订舱申请
direct payment valuation request /di'rekt, ˌvælju:'eiʃən/ 直接支付估价申请
interim application for payment /'intərim/ 临时支付申请
quantity valuation request 数量估价申请
request for quote /kwəut/ 报价申请
application for banker's draft 银行汇票申请书
application for banker's guarantee /ˌgærən'ti:/ 银行担保申请书
application for documentary credit /ˌdɔkju'mentəri/ 跟单信用证开证申请书
documentary credit application 跟单信用证申请书
application for goods control certificate 货物监管证书申请表
application for inspection certificate /in'spekʃən/ 商品检验申请表
application for phytosanitary certificate /'faitəuˌsænitəri/ 植物检疫申请表

application for certificate of origin 原产地证书申请表
application for export licence 出口许可证申请表
goods control certificate 货物监管证书
application for import licence 进口许可证申请表

16. ……收据
forwarder's warehouse receipt 货运代理人仓库收据
goods receipt 货物收据
goods receipt, carriage /ˈkærɪdʒ/ 承运人货物收据
mate's receipt /meits/ 大副收据
post receipt 邮政收据
receipt (Customs) 海关收据

17. ……提单
bill of lading copy /ˈkɔpi/ 副本提单
bill of lading original /əˈridʒinəl/ 正本提单
combined transport multimodal bill of lading 多式联运提单
empty container bill /ˈempti/ 空集装箱提单
forwarder's bill of lading 货运代理人提单
house bill of lading 全程提单
inland waterway bill of lading /ˈinlənd,ˈwɔːtəˌwei/ 内河提单
master bill of lading /ˈmɑːstə/ 主提单
tanker bill of lading /ˈtæŋkə/ 油轮提单
through bill of lading 直达提单

18. ……通知/通知书
advice of collection /ədˈvais,kəˈlekʃən/ 托收通知
advice of distribution of documents 单证分发通知
arrival notice(goods) /əˈraivəl,ˈnəutis/ 货物到达通知
calling forward notice /ˈkɔːliŋ/ 要求交货通知
customs delivery note 海关放行通知
delivery notice (goods) 交货通知
delivery notice(rail transport) 铁路运输交货通知
delivery release /riˈliːs/ 发货通知
dispatch advice 发运通知
documentary credit transfer advice /dɔkjuˈmentəri/ 跟单信用证转让通知
forwarder's advice to exporter /ikˈspɔːtə/ 货运代理给出口商的通知
forwarder's advice to import agent /ˈeidʒənt/ 货运代理给进口代理的通知
notice of circumstances preventing delivery (goods) /ˈsəːkəmstənsiz,priˈventiŋ/ 无法交货的通知
notice of circumstances preventing transport (goods) 无法运货通知
ready for dispatch advice /ˈredi/ 待运通知

remittance advice /ri'mitns/ 汇款通知
collection payment advice 托收支付通知书
credit advice 贷记通知书
debit advice 借记通知书
documentary credit acceptance advice /ək'septəns/ 跟单信用证承兑通知书
documentary credit amendment notification /ə'mendmənt,ˌnəutəfi'keiʃən/ 跟单信用证更改通知书
documentary credit negotiation advice /niˌgəuʃi:'eiʃən/ 跟单信用证议付通知书
documentary credit notification 跟单信用证通知书
documentary credit payment advice 跟单信用证支付通知书
extended credit advice /iks'tendid/ 扩展贷记通知书
preadvice of a credit /ˌpri:əd'vais/ 信用证预先通知书

19. ……运单

air waybill /ɛə,'weibil/ 空运单
cartage order(local transport) /'kɑ:tidʒ,'ləukəl/ 短途货运单
dispatch order 发运单
house waybill /haus/ 全程运单
master air waybill /'mɑ:stə/ 主空运单
rail consignment note (generic term) /reil,kən'sainmənt,nəut,dʒə'nerik,tə:m/ 铁路托运单（通用条款）
re-sending consignment note /ri:'sendiŋ/ 铁路运输退运单
road consignment note /rəud/ 公路托运单
sea waybill /si:/ 海运单
shipping note 托运单
substitute air waybill /'sʌbstitju:t/ 分空运单

20. ……证书/证明

certificate of analysis /ə'næləsis/ 分析证书
certificate of conformity /kən'fɔ:miti/ 一致性证书
certificate of origin 原产地证书
certificate of origin form GSP 普惠制原产地证书
certificate of quality 质量证书
certificate of quantity 数量证书
certificate of registry /'redʒistri:/ 船舶登记证书
combined certificate of value and origin 价值与原产地综合证书
de rat document /di:'reit/ 免于除鼠证书
EUR 1 certificate of origin EUR1 欧共体原产地证书
forwarder's certificate of transport 货运代理人运输证书
inspection certificate /in'spekʃən/ 商品检验证书
loadline document /ləud'lain/ 载重线证书

maritime declaration of health /ˈmæritaim,helθ/ 航海健康证书
mill certificate /mil/ 农产品加工厂证书
phytosanitary certificate /ˈfaitəuˌsænitəri/ 植物检疫证书
post receipt 家产品加工厂证书
preference certificate of origin /ˈprefərəns/ 优惠原产地证书
quota prior allocation certificate /ˈkwəutə,ˈpraiə,ˌæləˈkeiʃən/ 配额预分配证书
regional appellation certificate /ˈriːdʒənəl,ˌæpəˈleiʃən/ 地区名称证书
safety of equipment certificate /ˈseifti,iˈkwipmənt/ 设备安全证书
safety of radio certificate /ˈreidiəu/ 无线电台安全证书
safety of ship certificate 船舶安全证书
sanitary certificate /ˈsæniˌteri:/ 卫生检疫证书
veterinary certificate /ˈvetərəˌneri:/ 动物检疫证书
weight certificate 重量证书
forwarder's certificate of receipt 货运代理收据证明

21. ……其他

ATA carnet 暂准进口海关文件
previous Customs document/message /ˈpriːviəs/ 先前海关文件/报文
reversal of credit /riˈvəːsəl/ 贷记撤消
reversal of debit 借记撤消
agreement to pay /əˈgriːmənt/ 支付协议
banker's guarantee /ˌgærənˈtiː/ 银行担保
delivery just-in-time 按时交货
delivery verification certificate /ˌverəfiˈkeiʃən/ 交货核对证明
instructions for bank transfer 银行转账指示
letter of indemnity for non-surrender of bill of lading /inˈdemniti:, nɔnsəˈrendə/ 无提单提货保函
name/product plate /pleit/ 铭牌
offer/quotation /ˈɔfə,kwəuˈteiʃən/ 发盘/报价
party information /ˈpɑːti/ 参与方信息
passenger list /ˈpæsindʒə/ 乘客名单
price /sales catalogue /prais,seilz,ˈkætəlɔg/ 价格/销售目录
promissory note /ˈprɔmisəri/ 本票
quality data message 质量数据报文
query /ˈkwiəri/ 查询

二、其他物流术语(按英语字母排序排列)

accounting cost /əˈkauntiŋ/ 会计成本
accuracy audit /ˈækjurəsi,ˈɔːdit/ 正确性审计
Activity Based Classification /beist/ ABC 分类法

actual weight /ˈæktʃuəl/ 实际重量

added value 附加价值

after-sales service /ˈɑːftə- ˈseilz,ˈsəːvis/ 售后服务

aggregate shipments /ˈæɡriɡit,ˈʃipmənts/ 合并出货

air pollution /pəˈluʃən/ 空气污染

air freight 空运货件

arbitrage /ˈɑːbiˌtrɑːʒ/ 套利

asset recovery /ˈæset,riˈkʌvəri/ 资源回收

Automated Vehicle Identification /ˈɔːtəˌmeitid,aiˌdentifiˈkeiʃən/ 自动车辆识别

Automated Vehicle Location(AVL) /ləuˈkeiʃən/ 自动车辆位置

available capacity /əˈveiləbl,kəˈpæsiti/ 车辆承载能力

average clear stacking height /ˈævəridʒ,kliə/ 平均净堆叠高度

back haul /bæk,hɔːl/ 回程

backwardation /ˈbækwəˈdeiʃən/ 现货溢价

bar code label /ˈleibəl/ 条形码标签

bar code scanner /ˈskænə/ 条形码扫描机

base stock 基本存货

batch numbers /bætʃ,ˈnʌmbəz/ 批号

bay /bei/ 区域

bear /bɛə/ 卖空者

bear market 熊市

belt conveyor /belt,kənˈveiə/ 皮带式输送带

bi-directional read /bai-diˈrekʃənəl,riːd/ 双向读取

Bill of Materials(BOM) /məˈtiəriəlz/ 物料用量清单

broken carton /ˈbrəukən,ˈkɑːtən/ 已拆箱

broker /ˈbrəukə/ 经纪人

bulk carrier /ˈkæriə/ 散装运送业

bulk container 散装集装箱

bull /bul/ 买空者

bull market 牛市

cancellation charge /ˌkænsəˈleiʃən,tʃɑːdʒ/ 取消订单费用

cargo booking 预约托运

cargo inspection /inˈspekʃən/ 检查货物

cash discount /kæʃ,ˈdiskaunt/ 现金折扣

centralized dispatching /ˈsentrəˌlaizd,disˈpætʃiŋ/ 集中式派车

centralized procurement /prəˈkjuəmənt/ 集中采购

channel of distribution /ˈtʃænl/ 分销渠道

check in /tʃek/ 进货清点

claim /kleim/ 索赔

closed distribution system /kləuzd/ 封闭式配送系统
consumer physical distribution /kənˈsjuːmə,ˈfizikəl/ 消费者物流
cooperative buying /kəuˈɔpərətiv,ˈbaiiŋ/ 联合采购
cost control 成本控制
crane /krein/ 起重机
cubed out /kjuːbd/ 装载率
Customer Relationship Management(CRM) /riˈleiʃənʃip/ 客户关系管理
data warehousing 数据仓库
deadhead /ˈdedhed/ 空回头车
declining conveyor /diˈklainiŋ,kənˈveiə/ 倾斜式输送机
de-consolidation center /diːkənˌsɔliˈdeiʃən/ 分货中心
delivery costs 配送成本
delivery cycle 配送周期
delivery error 误送
delivery note 出货清单
delivery terminal 配送站
demand forecasting /diˈmɑːnd,ˈfɔːkɑːstiŋ/ 需求预测
depalletizer /diˈpæliˌtaizə/ 卸托盘机
design for logistics /diˈzain/ 为物流而设计
direct distribution /diˈrekt/ 直接配送
direct store delivery 直接配送到商店
dispatch area /ˈɛəriə/ 出货区
Distributed Resource Planning(DRP) /disˈtribjuːtid/ 分销资源计划
domestic intercity trucking /dəˈmestik,intəˈsitiː,ˈtrʌkiŋ/ 国内长途货运
domestic logistics 国内物流
double floor stacking /ˈdʌbl,flɔː/ 双层堆积
double pallets handling /ˈpælits,ˈhændliŋ/ 双托盘处理
double-pallet jack /dʒæk/ 双托盘设备
duty /ˈdjuːti/ 关税
economic stock /ikəˈnɔmik,stɔk/ 经济存货
electronic clearance /ilekˈtrɔnik,ˈkliərəns/ 电子通关
exclusive distribution /iksˈkluːsiv/ 独家分销
Executive Support System(ESS) /igˈzekjutiv/ 高层主管支持系统
fact tag /fækt,tæg/ 产品说明标签
factory price /ˈfæktəri/ 出厂价
firewall /ˈfaiəwɔːl/ 防火墙
fixed rack /fikst,ræk/ 固定式货架
flatbed trailer /ˈflætbed,ˈtreilə/ 平台拖车
fleet /fliːt/ 车(船)队

furniture removal carriers /ˈfəːnitʃə,riˈmuːvəl,ˈkæriəz/ 搬家公司
gateway /ˈgeitˌwei/ 转运站
Geographic Information System(GIS) /dʒiːəˈgræfik/ 地理信息系统
Global Positioning System(GPS) /ˈgləubəl,pəˈziʃəniŋ/ 全球定位系统
global logistics 全球物流
hand truck /hændˌtrʌk/ 手推车
handheld scanner /ˈhændˌheld/ 手提式扫描仪
heat insulating material /hiːt,ˈinsjuleitiŋ/ 隔热材料
hot tag /hɔt/ 紧急标签
Industrial Engineering(IE) /inˈdʌstriəl,ˌendʒiˈniəriŋ/ 工业工程
integrated logistics /ˈintigreitid/ 集成物流
Integrated Services Digital Network(ISDN) /ˈdidʒitəl,ˈnetwəːk/ 综合业务数据网
interchange terminal /intəˈtʃeindʒ/ 联运站
kanban system /ˈkɑːnbɑːn/ 看板系统
knowledge management /ˈnɔlidʒ/ 知识管理
label making machine /ˈleibəl,ˈmeikiŋ,məˈʃiːn/ 标签机
laser scanner /ˈleizə/ 激光扫描仪
logistician 物流师
logistics engineering 物流工程
loose packages /luːs/ 散装
make to order 订单生产
market orientation /ˈmɑːkit,ˌɔːrienˈteiʃən/ 市场导向
marking machine /ˈmɑːkiŋ/ 打标机
market share /ʃɛə/ 市场份额
materials handling equipment 物料搬运设备
middleware /ˈmidlwɛə/ 中间件
multi-story warehouse /ˈmʌltiˌstɔːri/ 多层仓库
net weight 净重
noise pollution /nɔiz,pəˈluʃən/ 噪音污染
number plate 牌照
on season /ˈsiːzən/ 旺季
Open DataBase Connectivity(ODBC) /ˈdeitəbeis,kənekˈtiviti/ 开放数据库互联
optical scanners /ˈɔptikəl/ 光学扫描仪
order processing /prəuˈsesiŋ/ 订单处理
Order Point System(OPS) /pɔint/ 定货点法
overload /ˌəuvəˈləud/ 超载
process center 处理中心
procurement /prəˈkjuəment/ 采购
quality control 质量控制

quarantine /ˈkwɔːrənˌtiːn/ 检疫
quotas /ˈkwəutəz/ 配额
rack /ræk/ 货架
regional distribution center /ˈriːdʒənəl/ 区域物流中心
retail selling /ˈriːteilˌˈseliŋ/ 零售
safety stock 安全存货
sealing machine /ˈsiːliŋˌməˈʃiːn/ 封装机
tank container /tæŋk/ 罐装集装箱
temporary labor /ˈtempərəriˌˈleibə/ 临时工
theory of Constraint(TOC) /ˈθiəriˌkənˈstreint/ 约束理论
vacuum packaging /ˈvækjuəm/ 真空包装
voice recognition /vɔisˌrekəgˈniʃən/ 语音识别
warehousing /ˈwɛəhauziŋ/ 仓储
waste /weist/ 废弃物
wholesalers /ˈhəulˌseiləz/ 批发商
zero stock /ˈziərəu/ 零库存

附录 C 物流业务中常见的英文省略语

ACA(American Collectors Association) /əˈmerikən,kəˈlektəz,əˌsəuʃiˈeiʃən/ 国际收账协会

ACEP(Automatic Consecutive Entrance Planning) /kənˈsekjutiv,ˈentrəns/ 自动连续补货计划

ADC(Automatic Data Collection) 自动数据采集

ADI(Acceptable Daily Intakes) /əkˈseptəbl,ˈdeili,ˈinteiks/ 每日允许摄入量

AFTA(Asian Free Trade Area) /ˈeiʃən,fri:,treid/ 亚洲自由贸易区或东盟自由贸易区

AGV(Automatic Guided Vehicle) /ˈɡaidid/ 自动导引车

AHV(Automatic Handling Vehicle) 智能化搬运车

AIAG(Automotive Industry Action Group) /ɔːtəˈməutiv,ˈækʃən,gru:p/ 汽车行业行动小组

ALIS(Advanced Label Imaging System) /ədˈvɑːnst,iˈmædʒiŋ/ 供顾客查询用的条形码包裹跟踪标签

AMTRAK(National Railroad Passenger Corporation) /ˈnæʃənəl,ˈreilrəud,ˈpæsindʒə,ˌkɔːpəˈreiʃən/ 美国国家铁路旅客公司

AOL(American OnLine) /ˌɔnˈlain/ 美国在线服务

APEC(Asia Pacific Economic Cooperation) /pəˈsifik,kəuˌɔpəˈreiʃən/ 亚太经济合作组织

APS(Advanced Planning System) 高级的(先进的)计划系统

AR(Automatic Replenishment) /riˈpleniʃmənt/ 自动化补充

AS 澳大利亚用于电器和非电器产品上的优质标志

ASN(Advance Ship Notice) /ˈnəutis/ 提前装船通知

ASP(Application Service Provider) /prəˈvaidə/ 应用服务提供商

ASRS(Automated Storage and Retrieval System) /riˈtriːvəl/ 自动化存取系统

ATA(Temporary Admission 的字首混合组成) /ˈtempərəri,ədˈmiʃən/ 货物暂准进出口通关制度

AT&T(American Telegraph & Telephone) /ˈteliˌɡræf,ˈtelifəun/ 美国电话电报公司

ATM(Air Traffic Management) 空中交通管理系统

B2A(Business to Administration) /ədˌminisˈtreiʃən/ 企业与行政机构的电子商务

B2B(Business to Business) 企业与企业的电子商务
B2C(Business to Consumer) 企业与消费者的电子商务
B2E(Business to Employee) /ˌemplɔi'i:/ 企业对员工的电子商务
BBS(Bulletin Board System) /'bulitin,bɔ:d/ 电子广告牌系统
BC(Bar Code) 条码
BEB 英国用于家用电器设备上的标志
BIS(Bank for International Settlements) /'setlmənts/ 国际清算银行
B/L(Bill of Lading) 提单
B/N(Booking Note) 托运单或订舱单
BPR(Business Process Reengineering) /ˌri:endʒi'niəriŋ/ 业务流程重组
BSE(Bovine Spongiform Encephalopathy) /'bəuˌvain,'spʌndʒifɔ:m,enˌsefə'lɔpəθi/ 疯牛病
BTO(Built To Order) /bilt/ 以顾客订货为基准的生产模式
3C(Customer,Competition,Change) /kɔmpi'tiʃən/ 顾客、竞争、变化
C2A(Consumer to Administration) 消费者对政府的电子商务
CAA(the Clean Air Act) /kli:n,ækt/ 美国的清洁空气法
CAA(Civil Aeronautics Authority) /'sivl,eərə'nɔ:tiks,ɔ:'θɔriti/ 美国民用航空局
C2B(Consumer to Business) 消费者对企业的电子商务
CAB(Civil Aeronautics Board) 美国民用航空委员会
C2C(Consumer to Consumer) 消费者对消费者的电子商务
CAD(Computer Aided Design) /'eidid,di'zain/ 计算机辅助设计
CAE(Computer Aided Engineering) /ˌendʒi'niəriŋ/ 计算机辅助工程
CALS(Computer Aided Acquisition and Logistic Support) /ækwi'ziʃən/ 计算机辅助采购及物流支持
CAM(Computer Aided Manufacture) /'mænju'fæktʃə/ 计算机辅助制造
CAO(Computer Aided Ordering) /'ɔ:dəriŋ/ 计算机辅助订货
CAPP(Computer Aided Process Planning) 计算机辅助工艺设计
CAU(Central Asian Economic Union) /'sentrəl,'ju:njən/ 中亚经济共同体
CBD(Central Business District) /'distrikt/ 中央商务区
CCCP 俄罗斯用于产品上的认证标志,表示产品符合安全标准
CCR(Class Cargo Rat) 航空运输的等级货物运价
C/D(Customs Declaration) 报关单
CE 欧盟用于机械产品上的标志,表示产品性能安全
CFR(Cost and Freight) 成本加运费价
CFS(Container Freight Station) 集装箱货运站
CIF(Cost Insurance and Freight) 成本加保险费加运费价
CIMS(Computer Integrated Manufacturing System) /'intigreitid/ 计算机集成制造系统
CIP(Carriage and Insurance Paid to) 运费、保险费付至(指定目的地)价
CIQ(China Inspection and Quarantine) /in'spekʃən,'kwɔ:rənˌti:n/ 中国检验检疫
CLO(Chief Logistics Officer) /tʃi:f,'ɔfisə/ 物流主管

CLP(Container Load Plan) 集装箱装箱单
CMI(Committee Maritime International) /kəˈmiti/ 国际海事委员会
CNN(Cable News Network) /ˈkeibl/ 美国有线新闻网
CNNIC(China Internet Network Information Center) 中国互联网络信息中心
CNS(Communication Navigation Surveillance) /kəˌmjuːniˈkeiʃən, næviˈgeiʃən, səˈveiləns/ 航空通讯导航监视
C.O(Certificate of Origin) 一般原产地证
COA(Contract of Affreightment) /kənˈtrækt, əˈfreitmənt/ 包运租船
COC(Carrier Owner Container) /ˈkæriə, ˈəunə/ 承运人的集装箱
COD(Cash on Delivery) /kæʃ/ 交货收款
CPT(Carriage Paid to) 运费付至(指定目的地)
CSA 加拿大的认证标志,表示产品安全合格
CTM(Cargo Transfer Manifest) /ˈmænifest/ 航空转运舱单
CTN/CTNS(Carton/Cartons) /ˈkɑːtənz/ 纸箱
CY(Container Yard) 集装箱堆场
D/A(Document against Acceptance) /əˈgeinst, əkˈseptəns/ 承兑交单
DAF(Delivered at Frontier) /ˈfrʌnˌtiə/ 边境交货价
DDC(Destination Delivery Charge) /ˌdestiˈneiʃən/ 目的港交货费
DDP(Delivered Duty Paid) /ˈdjuːti/ 完税后交货价
DDU(Delivered Duty Unpaid) /ʌnˈpeid/ 未完税交货价
DEQ(Delivered Ex Quay) /eks, kiː/ 目的港码头交货价
DES(Delivered Ex Ship) 目的港船上交货价
DG(Dangerous Goods) /ˈdeindʒərəs/ 危险物品
DIN 德国用于电子产品上的标志,表示产品合格
DL/DLs(Dollar/Dollars) /ˈdɔləz/ 美元
DN(Domain Name) /dəuˈmein/ 域名
DOC(Document) 文件、单据
D/O(Delivery Order) 提货单
DOT(Department of Transportation) 运输部
DOZ/DZ(Dozen) /ˈdʌzn/ 一打
DPD(Direct Plant Delivery) /plɑːnt/ 直接工厂送货
DPS(Data Pick System) 数字化分拣系统
D/R(Dock Receipt) /dɔk/ 站场收据
DSD(Direct Store Delivery) 直接配送到商店
DSS(Decision Support System) /diˈsiʒən/ 决策支持系统
EA(Each) 每个,各
EAN(European Article Number) 欧洲条码系统
EANCOM(EAN Communication) /kəˌmjuːniˈkeiʃən/ 电子通信标准
EB(Electronic Business) 电子商务

附录 C
Appendix C

EC(Electronic Commercial) 电子商务

EC/EEC(European Economic Community) /kəˈmjuːniti/ 欧共体

ECGD(Export Credits Guarantee Department) /ˌgærənˈtiː, diˈpɑːtmənt/ 英国出口信用担保部门

EDI(Electronic Data Interchange) 电子数据交换

EFTA(European Free Trade Association) /əˌsəuʃiˈeiʃən/ 欧洲自由贸易协会

EMS(Express Mail Special) /iksˈpres, meil, ˈspeʃəl/ 特快传递

ERC(Empty Return Charges) /ˈempti, riˈtəːn, ˈtʃɑːdʒiz/ 空箱回运箱费

ETA(Estimate Time of Arrival) /ˈestimeit/ 预计到达时间

EXP(Export) 出口

FAA(Federal Aeronautics Administration) /ˈfedərəl, ˌeərəˈnɔːtiks/ 美国联邦航空管理局

FAC(Facsimile) /fækˈsiməliː/ 传真

FAO (Food and Agriculture Organization of the United Nation) /ˈægrikʌltʃə, ˌɔːgənaiˈzeiʃən, juːˈnaitid, ˈneiʃən/ 联合国粮农组织

FAQ(Frequently Asked Questions) /ˈfriːkwəntli/ 交易说明

FCL(Full Container Load) 整箱

FDA(Food and Drug Administration) 美国食品与药物管理局

FDI(Foreign Direct Investment) /ˈfɔrin, inˈvestmənt/ 外国直接投资

FedEx(Federal Express) 联邦快递

FIATA (International Federation of Freight Forwarders Associations) /ˌfedəˈreiʃən, ˈfɔːwədəz, əˌsəuʃiˈeiʃənz/ 国际货运代理协会联合会

FMD(Foot & Mouth Disease) /diˈziːz/ 口蹄疫

FMS(Flexible Manufacturing System) /ˈfleksəbl, ˌmænjuˈfæktʃəriŋ/ 柔性制造系统

FOB(Free on Board) 船上交货,离岸价

FTA(Canada—United States Free Trade Agreement) /ˈkænədə, treid, əˈgriːmənt/ 美加自由贸易协定

FTP(File Transfer Protocol) /fail, trænsˈfəː, ˈprəutəˌkɔːl/ 文件传输协议

3G(Third Generation) /ˌdʒenəˈreiʃən/ 第三代移动网络

GATT(General Agreement on Tariffs and Trade) /ˈdʒenərəl, ˈtærifs/ 关税与贸易总协定

G2B(Government to Business) 政府对企业的电子商务

GCR(General Cargo Rate) 航空运输的一般货物运价

GDP(Gross Domestic Product) /grəus, dəˈmestik/ 国内生产总值

GMT(Greenwich Mean Time) /ˈgrinidʒ, miːn/ 世界时间标准

GNP(Gross National Product) 国民生产总值

G. S. P. (Generalized System of Preferences) /ˈdʒenərəlaizd, ˈprefərənsiz/ 普惠制

GTN(Global Transport Net) /ˈgləubəl/ 全球运输网

G. W. (Gross Weight) /weit/ 毛重

H-B/L(House B/L) 分提单

HKANA(Hong Kong Article Numbering Association) 香港货品编码协会

HKQMARK 香港的认证标志,表示产品优良
HAWB(House Air Waybill) 航空分运单
IACS(International Association of Classification Societies) /sə'saiətiz/ 国际船级社协会
IATA(International Air Transport Association) 国际航空运输协会
ICAD(International Civil Aviation Organization) /ˌeiviˈeiʃən,ˌɔːɡənaiˈzeiʃən/ 国际民用航空组织
ICC(International Chamber of Commerce) /ˈtʃeimbə,ˈkɔməːs/ 美国的州际商会
ICP(Internet Content Provider) /ˈkɔntent,prəˈvaidə/ 互联网内容提供商
ICS(International Chamber of Shipping) 国际航运分会
I/D(In Dial) /ˈdaiəl/ 被动式存送
IDEA(International Data Exchange Association) 国际数据交换协会
IMM(International Monetary Market) /ˈmʌnitəri/ 国际货币市场
IMO(International Marine Organization) /məˈriːn/ 国际海事组织
IMP(Import) 进口
INCOTERMS(International Commercial Terms) /təːmz/ 国际贸易术语解释通则
INT(International) 国际的
INV(Invoice) 发票
IP(Internet Protocol) 互联网通讯协议
ISO(International Standard Organization) /ˈstændəd/ 国际标准化组织
ISP(Internet Service Provider) /prəˈvaidə/ 互联网接入服务商
ITS(Intelligent Transport System) /inˈtelidʒənt/ 智能运输系统
JAS 日本用于林木产品及食品上的认证标志,表示产品优良
JIS 日本用于工业产品上的认证标志,表示产品合格
JWS 国际羊毛局的认证标志,表示羊毛质量符合国际羊毛局的要求
LAN(Local Area Network) /ˈləukəl/ 局域网
L/C(Letter of Credit) 信用证
LDSS(Logistics Decision Support System) 物流决策支持系统
LTL(Less-than-Truck-Load) 零担运输
M 或 MED(Medium) /ˈmiːdjəm/ 中等,中级的
MAWB(Master Air Waybill) 航空主运单
MAX(Maximum) /ˈmæksiməm/ 最大的、最大限度的
MC(Motor Carrier) /ˈməutə,ˈkæriə/ 指美国汽车承运人
MIN(Minimum) /ˈminiməm/ 最小的,最低限度
MT 或 M/T(Metric Ton) /ˈmetrik,tʌn/ 公吨
MTD(Multimodal Transport Document) /ˌmʌltiˈməudəl/ 多式联运单据
MTO(Multimodal Transport Operator) /ˈɔpəreitə/ 多式联运经营人
M/V(Merchant Vessel) /ˈməːtʃənt,ˈvesəl/ 商船
NAFTA(North American Free Trade Agreement) 北美自由贸易协定
NASA(National Aeronautics and Space Administration) /ˌɛərəˈnɔːtiks,ədˌminisˈtreiʃən/

美国国家航空与空间管理局

NCPDM(National Council of Physical Distribution Management) /ˈkaunsl/ 美国物流管理协会

NF 法国用于电器及电器产品上的标志,表示产品符合安全要求

NTPSC(National Transportation Policy Study Commission) /ˈpɔləsi,kəˈmiʃən/ 美国国家运输政策研究委员会

N. W. (Net Weight) 净重

OAU(Organization of African Unity) /ˈæfrikən,ˈjuːniti/ 非洲统一组织

O/D(Out Dial) /ˈdaiəl/ 主动式存送

OECD (Organization for Economic Cooperation and Development) /kəuˌɔpəˈreiʃən,diˈveləpmənt/ 经济合作与发展

OEM(Original Equipment Manufacturer) /əˈridʒinəl,ˌmænjuˈfæktʃərə/ 原始设备制造商

3P(Pollution Prevention Pays) /pəˈluʃən,priˈvenʃən,peiz/ 防污染投资

4P(Product/Promotion/Price/Place) /prəˈməuʃən/ 产品、促销、价格、渠道

PCE/PCS(Piece/Pieces) 只、个、支等

PCT(Percent) /pəˈsent/ 百分比

PD(Physical Distribution) 货物配送

PDT(Portable Data Terminal) /ˈpɔːtəbl,ˈtəːminəl/ 便携式数据终端设备

PIM(Physical Inventory Management) 实物库存管理

PKG(Package) 一包,一捆,一扎,一件等

P/L(Packing List) 装箱单、明细表

PO(Purchase Order) /ˈpəːtʃəs/ 采购订货

POD(Proof of Delivery) /pruːf/ 交付凭证(空运)

POQ(Period Order Quantity) /ˈpiərəd/ 定期订货批量

POS(Point of Sale) 销售点

PR 或 PRC(Price) 价格

PSI(Pre—shipment Inspection) /ˈʃipmənt,inˈspekʃən/ 装船前检查

PSS(Peak Season Surcharges) /piːk,ˈsəːtʃɑːdʒiz/ 旺季附加费

PUR(Purchase) 购买、购货

PVC(Poly Vinyl Chloride) /ˈpɔli,ˈvainəl,ˈklɔːraid/ 聚氯乙烯

QTSP(Quality Technology Service Price) 物流需求价

REF(Reference) /ˈrefrəns/ 参考、查价

RFP(Request for Proposal) /prəˈpəuzəl/ 目标说明书

RMB(Renminbi) 人民币

ROA(Returns on Asset) /riˈtəːnz,ˈæset/ 资金收益率

ROI(Returns on Investment) /inˈvestmənt/ 投资报酬率

RPS(Road Package System) 包裹速递系统

SS(safety Stock) 安全储备

S. S(Steamship) /ˈstiːmʃip/ 船运

S-B/L(Sea-B/L) 船公司签发的提单

S/C(Sales Contract) /kən'trækt/ 销售确认书

SCR(Special Cargo Rate) 航空运输的特种货物运价

S/F(Store and Forward) 主动式存送

SL(Service Level) 服务水平

S/M(Shipping Marks) 装船标记

S/O(Shipping Order) 装货单

SOC(Shipper Owner Container) 货主的集装箱

SOLE(Society of Logistics Engineers) /sə'saiəti,ˌendʒi'niəz/ 全美后勤工程师学会

SPC(Special Charger) /'speʃəl,'tʃɑːdʒə/ 特别附加费

SPS(Sanitary and Phytosanitary) /'sæniˌteriː,'faitəuˌsænitəri/ 实施动植物卫生检疫措施协议

S/R(Store and Retrieve) /ri'triːv/ 被动式存货

STL.(Style) /stail/ 式样、款式、类型

T 或 LTX 或 TX(Telex) /'telˌeks/ 电传

T/T(Telegraphic Transfer) /ˌteli'græfik/ 电汇

T/T(Transit Time) /'trænsit/ 航程

TTL(_Total) 总共

TBT(Technical Barriers to Trade) /'teknikəl,'bæriəz/ 技术性贸易壁垒协议

TCP(Transmission Control Protocol) /trænz'miʃən/ 网上传输控制协议

TDCC(Transportation Date Coordinating Committee) /kəu'ɔːdineitiŋ,kə'miti/ 运输数据协调委员会

THC(Terminal Handling Charges) 终点站搬运费

T/S(Trans-Ship) 转船,转运

UCC(Uniform Code Council Inc) /'juːnifɔːm,'kaunsl/ 美国统一编码委员会

UCS(Uniform Communication Standards) /'stændədz/ 统一通信标准

UDP(User Datagram Protocol) /'juːzə,'deitəgræm/ 用户数据协议

UL 美国电器产品的安全认证标志

UPC(Universal Product Code) /ˌjuːni'vəːsəl/ 通用产品标码或代码

UPS(United Parcel Service) /'pɑːsəl/ 联合速递公司

VAL(Value Added Logistics) 增值物流服务

VAN(Value Added Networks) 商业增值网

W(With) 具有

W/O(Without) 没有

WTO(World Trade Organization) /ˌɔːgənai'zeiʃən/ 世界贸易组织

W/T(Weight Ton) /weit,tʌn/ 重量吨(即货物收费以重量计费)

YAS(Yard Surcharges) /'səːˌtʃɑːdʒiz/ 码头附加费

附录 D　国际物流贸易术语

1. 启运术语：EXW（Ex Works 工厂交货……指定地）
2. 主要运费未付术语：1）FCA（Free Carrier 交货承运人……指定地点）
   2）FAS（Free Alongside Ship 船边交货）
   3）FOB（Free on Board 装运港船上交货）
3. 主要运费已付术语：1）CFR（Cost and Freight 成本加运费）
   2）CIF（Cost Insurance and Freight 成本保险费加运费）
   3）CPT（Carriage Paid To 运费付至目的地）
   4）CIP（Carriage and Insurance Paid To 运费、保险费付至目的地）
4. 货物到达术语：1）DAF（Delivered at Frontier 边境交货）
   2）DES（Delivered Ex Ship 目的港船上交货）
   3）DEQ（Delivered Ex Quay 目的港码头交货）
   4）DDU（Delivered Duty Unpaid 目的地交货关税未付）
   5）DDP（Delivered Duty Paid 目的地交货关税已付）

附录 E 部分物流外贸单据样本

一、英文海运提单样本及中文解释

Table 1　Bill of Lading

1. SHIPPER(托运人)	B/L NO.
2. CONSIGNEE(收货人)	BILL OF LADING
3. NOTIFY PARTY(被通知人)	ORIGINAL(正本)
4. PRE-CARRIAGE BY(前段运输)	5. PLACE OF RECEIPT(收据地)
6. OCEAN VESSEL VOY. NO.(航次)	7. PORT OF LOADING(装货港)
8. PORT OF DISCHARGE(卸货港)	9. PLACE OF DELIVERY(送货地)

MARKS & NOS. (唛头)	NO. OF CONTAINERS OR PACKAGES (集装或包装件数)	DESCRIPTION OF GOODS (货名)	G.W. (毛重)	MEA. (尺码)
		TOTAL:		

| 10. TOTAL NUMBER OF CONTAINERS AND/OR PACKAGE(IN WORD)SAY TOTAL
(集装或包装件数) ||||||

11. PREPAID (运费预付)	PREPAID AT (预付地点)	COLLECT (领取)	PAYABLE AT (付款地点)	PLACE AND DATE OF ISSUE (签发提单的地点和时间)
NO. OF ORIGINAL(正本提单的份数)				SIGNATURE(签发/字)

二、英文航空运单样本及解释

Table 2　Airway Bill

Shipper's name and address 1)(发货人姓名和地址)	NOT NEGOTIABLE　　中国民航　　CAAC AIR WAYBILL(AIR CONSIGNMENT NOTE) ISSUED BY THE CIVIL AVIATION ADMINISTRATION OF CHINA BEIJING CHINA
Consignee's name and address 2)(收货人姓名和地址)	It is agreed that the goods described herein are accepted in apparent good order and condition（except as noted）for carriage subject to the conditions of contract on the reverse hereof, all goods may be carried by any other means, including road or any other carrier unless specific contrary instructions are given hereon by the shipper. The shipper's attention is drawn to the notice concerning carrier's limitation of liability. Shipper may increase such limitation of liability by declaring a higher value of carriage and paying a supplemental charge if required.
Issuing Carrier's Agent Name and City 3)(承运人代理的名称和所在城市)	
Agents IATA Code Account No. 4)5)(代理人的IATA代号、账号)	
Airport of Departure(Add. of First Carrier) and Requested Routing 6)(始发站机场及所要求的航线)	Accounting Information 7)(支付信息)
To,By first carrier,To,By,To,By,Currency,Declared Value for Carriage,Declared Value for Customs 8)　9)　10)　11)　12)　13)　14)　15)　16)　（去往、第一承运人、去往、承运人、去往、货币、运输声明价值、海关声明价值）	
Airport of Flight/Date,Amount of INSURANCE—If carrier offers insurance and such insurance　17)18) 19)(航班及日期、保险金额) Destination Insurance is requested in accordance with the conditions thereof indicating amount to be insured in figures in box marked "Amount of Insurance"	
Handling Information　20)(操作信息)	
No. of Pieces,G. W.,Rate Class,Chargeable Weight,Rate/Charge,Total,Nature & Quantity of Goods　21) 22)　23)　24)　25)　26)　27)(货物件数、毛重、运价等级、计费重量、运价、运费总额、货物的品名和数量)	
Prepaid Weight charge,Collect Other Charges　28)　29)(预付重量计价运费、其他运费到付)	

Valuation Charge 30)(声明价值表)
Total Other Charges Due Carrier, Signature of Shipper or his agent   31)(需要付与承运人的其他费用合计金额、托运人或其货运代理人签字、盖章)
Total Prepaid   32)(预付货物运费总额) Total Collect 33)(到付货物运费总额) 　　Executed on _____ at _____ Signature (填开日期) 　　Currency Conversion Rates CC Charges in des. Currency of issuing 　　　　　　　　　　　　　　　　　　　　　　　Carrier or as Agent 34)　 35)　（货币换算及目的地机场收费纪录）
For Carrier's Use Charges at Destination Total Collect Charges AIR WAYBILL NUMBER Only at Destination 36)　 37)　 38)(给承运人费用、在目的地总到付费用、仅仅在目的地)

三、保险单样本及解释

Table 3　Insurance Policy

中国太平洋保险公司广州分公司

CHINA PACIFIC INSURANCE COMPANY LIMITED

No　　　保险单　　　　　　　　　　　　　　保险单号次

　　INSURANCE POLICY　　　　　　　　POLICY NO. PNJ001/

中国太平洋保险公司(以下简称本公司)根据_____

_____(以下简称被保险人)的要求,由被保险人向本公司缴付约定的保险费,按照本保险单承保险别和背面所载条款于下列特款承保下述货物运输保险,特立本保险单。

　　THIS POLICY OF INSURANCE WITNESSES THAT CHINA PACIFIC INSURANCE COMPANY LIMITED (HEREINAFTER CALLED " THE COMPANY " AT THE REQUEST OF... HEREINAFTER CALLED " THE INSURED ") AND IN CONSIDERATION OF THE AGREED PREMIUM PAYING TO THE COMPANY BY THE INSURED, UNDERTAKES TO INSURE THE UNDERMENTIONED GOODS IN TRANSPORTATION SUBJECT TO THE CONDITIONS OF THIS POLICY AS PER THE CLAUSES PRINTED OVERLEAF AND OTHER SPECIAL CLAUSES ATTACHED HEREON.

标　记 MARKS & NO. S	包装、数量及保险货物项目 QUANTITY AND DESCRIPTION OF GOODS	保 险 金 额 AMOUNT INSURED

总保险金额：
TOTAL AMOUNT INSURED：_____

保费　　　　　　　　　　　　　　　　费率
PREMIUM _____　RATE _____

装载运输工具
PER CONVEYANCE S. S _____

开航日期　　　　　　　　　　　　　　自
SLGON OR ABT：_____　FROM _____

至
TO _____

承保险别：
CONDITIONS：

所保货物，如遇出险，本公司凭第一正本保险单及其他有关证件给付赔款。所保货物，如发生本保险单项下负责赔偿的损失或事故，应立即通知本公司下述代理人查勘。

CLAIMS, IF ANY, PAYABLE ON SURRENDER OF THE FIRST ORIGINAL OF THE POLICY TOGETHER WITH OTHER RELEVANT DOCUMENTS. IN THE EVENT OF ACCIDENT WHEREBY LOSS OR DAMAGE MAY RESULT IN A CLAIM UNDER THIS POLICY, IMMEDIATE NOTICE APPLYING FOR SURVEY MUST BE GIVEN TO THE COMPANY'S AGENT AS MENTIONED HEREUNDER：

　　　　　　　　　　　　　　　　中国太平洋保险公司广州分公司
　　　　　　　　　　　　　　CHINA PACIFIC INSURANCE CO., LTD.
　　　　　　　　　　　　　　　　　　GUANGZHOU BRANCH

赔款偿付地点
CLAIM PAYABLE AT _____

日期：
DATE：_____

地址：　　　　　　　　　　　　　　　　　　_____
ADDRESS：_____　　　GENERAL MANAGER

TEL：_____　FAX：_____

四、装箱单样本及解释

Table 4　Packing List

ISSUER:（出票人全称与详细地址）	装箱单 Packing List	
TO:	INVOICE NUMBER:（发票号码） DATE:（发票日期）	TRANSPORT DETAILS: （运输细节）
MARKS & NO. （唛头及件号）　QUANTITY （件数）　DESCRIPTION OF GOODS （货物描述）　G.W. （毛重）　N.W. （净重）　MEASUREMENT （尺码）		
SIGNATURE:（出票人盖章和签字）		

五、商业发票样本及解释

Table 5　Commercial Invoice

SELLER/EXPORTER/ ISSUER: （卖方/出口商/出票人）	商业发票 Commercial Invoice	
TO:	INVOICE NUMBER:（发票号码） DATE（发票日期）:	TRANSPORT DETAILS: （运输细节）
MARKS & NO. （唛头及件号）　QUANTITY （数量）　DESCRIPTION OF GOODS （货物描述）　UNIT PRICE （商品的单价）　AMOUNT （总价值）		
SIGNATURE:（签章）		

六、原产地证书样本及解释

Table 6　Certificate of Origin

1. EXPORTER(出口方)(出口公司的详细地址、名称和国家/地区名。)	CERTIFICATE NO. 20020264412(证书编号) CERTIFICATE OF ORIGIN OF THE PEOPLE'S REPUBLIC OF CHINA
2. CONSIGNEE(收货方)(收货人的名称、地址和国家/地区名	
3. MEANS OF TRANSPORT AND ROUTE(运输方式和路线)(目的港和装运港、运输方式。如果转运,应注明转运地)	5. FOR CERTIFYING AUTHORITY ONLY (签证机构用栏)
4. COUNTRY/REGION OF DESTINATION(目的地国家)应与最终收货人或最终目的港国家一致,不能填写中间商国家名称。)	

6. MARKS AND NUMBER(运输标志)(添写唛头)e.g. A.T.L MADE IN CHINA C/NO.1-52	7. NUMBER AND KIND OF PACKAGING; DESCRIPTION OF GOODS(商品名称、包装数量及种类)	8. H.S. CODE(商品编码)(填写 H.S. 编码,与报关单一致)e.g. 85.28	9. QUANTITY(数量) e.g. 620PCS	10. NUMBER AND DATE OF INVOICES(发票号码及日期)

11. DECLARATION BY THE EXPORTER(出口方声明)(出口人的名称、申报地点及日期)	12. CERTIFICATION(发证机构签章、签名)

附录 F 试卷

物流专业《物流英语》理论期中考试用卷

考试时间：100 分钟

注：本卷适用于中、高职物流班　共 100 分

一、单项选择（共 10 小题，每题 2 分，共 20 分）

(　　)1. — Have you heard that _____ has become a hot career(职业)?
　　— Of course. Now I am learning logistics.
　　A. warehousing　　　　　　　　B. logistics
　　C. packaging　　　　　　　　　D. transportation

(　　)2. Logistics is the part of the _____ chain process.
　　A. supplier　　B. supply　　C. supplies　　D. supplied

(　　)3. Customer service is the _____ of the logistics system.
　　A. out　　B. output　　C. outer　　D. put

(　　)4. _____ collects data in real time.
　　A. Warehouse　　　　　　　　　B. Inventory
　　C. Distribution center　　　　　　D. Transportation

(　　)5. _____ refers to（指的是）places（地方）where goods can be stored for a period of time（储存一段时间）.
　　A. Transfer　　B. Freight　　C. Handle　　D. Warehousing

(　　)6. The three basic components of the warehousing（仓储的基本组成）are _____, equipment and people.
　　A. rack　　B. picking　　C. shipping　　D. warehouse

(　　)7. Packaging is to _____ the goods.
　　A. protect　　B. move　　C. damage　　D. transport

(　　)8. Industrial package(工业包装) is also the _____ package.
　　A. exterior　　B. consumer　　C. interior　　D. marketing

(　　)9. Distribution includes many operations for the items, such as picking, _____ and so on.

   A．processing B．packaging C．dividing D．all above

( )10．Logistics can be classified as _____．

   A．Supply Logistics   B．Production Logistics

   C．Returned Logistics   D．all above

二、阅读理解（共10小题，每题2分，共20分）

  通读下面的短文，掌握其大意。然后，从每小题的四个选项中选出可填入相应空白处的最佳选项。

（一）

  I am Cheng Lin. I am from Henan. I want to live in a large city. I came to this technical school(技校) last month. I have been studying logistics for a month. All our teachers are hardworking(勤奋) and we students study hard every day. With the help of our teachers, I have learned how important logistics is all over the world. There are so many contents(内容) in logistics. I think I should study harder on this subject(课程) and I will master it little by little(逐渐地). I like everything here. In the future I can do more for our country.

  根据短文内容选择问题最合适的答语。

( )1) Tom：What does Cheng Lin do?

   Jane：She is a(an) _____．

   A．teacher B．adult C．child D．student

( )2) Tom：How does Cheng Lin like logistics?（觉得物流怎么样）

   Jane：_____．

   A．Hard B．Easy C．Interesting D．Important

( )3) Tom：What does she want to do in the future?

   Jane：She will _____．

   A．be a logistics manager   B．be a logistics agent

   C．do more work for herself   D．make great contribution to country

( )4) Tom：What does Cheng Lin major in?

   Jane：She majors in _____．

   A．motor repair specialty   B．electrical contractor professional

   C．computer   D．logistics

( )5) Tom：Does Cheng Lin like her school?

   Jane：_____．

   A．No   B．Sorry, I don't know

   C．Yes, she doesn't   D．Yes

（二）

  (Mary is making a telephone call to order a ring（戒指）she has seen on TV)

  Clerk：Hello, this is the sales assistant speaking.

  Mary：Hello, I saw a ring in your commercial program on TV yesterday. May I order that ring by phone?

Clerk: Sure. Do you know the sales number?
Mary: Yes, it's 4805. A 24k gold ring.
Clerk: Hold on, please. Let me check it for you. Yes, we have this ring in store. It's 900 yuan. You can place an order now. Please tell me your name and address.
Mary: That's Mary, No. 60 Xinhua Street.
Clerk: Mary, No. 60 Xinhua Street. You need the ring under the sales number 4805.
Mary: When can I get it? Saturday will be convenient.
Clerk: Saturday is ok, I will inform the delivery department.
Mary: Do you charge for the delivery?
Clerk: Yes, we will charge 10 yuan for the delivery.
Mary: How will I pay?
Clerk: You may pay in cash to our delivery man on Saturday.
Mary: Thank you.

( )6) — What does Mary want to order?
— _____.
  A. A ring   B. A necklace   C. An earring   D. A bracelet

( )7) — Where did she see the ring?
— _____.
  A. At home   B. On TV   C. In the shop   D. In the market

( )8) — How much is the ring?
— _____.
  A. 100 yuan   B. 200 yuan   C. 900 yuan   D. 10 yuan

( )9) — Does the clerk charge for the delivery?
— _____.
  A. No   B. I don't know
  C. The dialogue doesn't say   D. Yes

( )10) — How will Mary pay to the delivery man?
— _____.
  A. In cash   B. In check
  C. With the credit card   D. In the E-currency

三、物流术语英汉翻译(共10小题,每题2分,共20分)

1. value-added service   _____
2. logistics system   _____
3. customer service   _____
4. consumer package   _____
5. finished products   _____
6. 仓储   _____
7. 配送中心   _____

8. 保护货物 _____
9. 库存管理 _____
10. 物流决策 _____

四、匹配题(共 5 小题,每题为 2 分,共 10 分)

从第Ⅱ栏里找到与第一栏一致的翻译

Ⅰ	Ⅱ
1. order picking	A. 舱位
2. end-user	B. 逆向物流
3. shipping space	C. 安全库存
4. safe inventory	D. 订单拣选
5. reverse distribution	E. 最终用户

1—( ) 2—( ) 3—( ) 4—( ) 5—( )

五、回答问题(共 5 小题,每题为 2 分,共 10 分)

1. — Can packaging help the sales?
   _____

2. — Does warehousing support production, too?
   _____

3. — What is the meaning of the physical movements of goods from the supplier to the receiver in Chinese Logistics Terms?
   _____

4. — What activities does warehousing involve(涉及)?
   _____

5. — How many steps of operation flow are there in the distribution center?
   _____

六、英汉翻译题(共 5 小题,每题为 2 分,共 10 分)

1. Logistics is a unique global pipeline.
   _____

2. Consumer packaging is also referred to the interior package, or marketing package.
   _____

3. We can provide you with a variety of goods inventory.
   _____

4. 配送中心处理大量的增值活动。(perform)
   _____

5. 物流管理将会发展为全球供应链管理。(evolve to)
   _____

物流专业《物流英语》理论期末考试用卷

考试时间:100 分钟

注:本卷适用于中、高职物流班　共 100 分

一、单项选择(共 10 小题,每题 2 分,共 20 分)

( )1. The transportation of international trading is carried out(执行) in _____.
   A. containers　　B. wooden box　　C. small box　　D. metal

( )2. Container freight stations is _____ for short.
   A. LCL　　　　B. CFSs　　　　C. FCL　　　　D. TEUs

( )3. The port of discharge also means _____ port.
   A. the loading　　B. the main　　C. the unloading　　D. the storage

( )4. An _____ is a form of B/L used for the air transport of goods.
   A. certificate of origin　　　　B. packing list
   C. B/L　　　　　　　　　　　D. air waybill

( )5. _____ is the physical movement(物体移动) of goods from one place to another place.
   A. Inventory　　　　　　　　B. warehouse
   C. Packaging　　　　　　　　D. Transportation

( )6. IT is short for _____.
   A. communication technology　　B. computer technology
   C. information technology　　　　D. database technology

( )7. One of the most important documents in _____ trade is the bill of lading.
   A. maritime　　　　　　　　B. road
   C. air　　　　　　　　　　　D. domestic(国内的)

( )8. Companies use _____ as a driver to become more efficient(效率高的) and more responsive(易受控制的).
   A. container　　B. purchase　　C. distributor　　D. information

( )9. _____ transportation is quick(快捷).
   A. Railway　　B. Airway　　C. Pipeline　　D. Road

( )10. _____ must be accurate, accessible, timely and of the right kind.
   A. Transportation　B. Information　C. Warehousing　D. Inventory

二、阅读理解(共 10 小题,每题 2 分,共 20 分)

通读下面的短文和对话,掌握其大意。然后,从每小题的四个选项中选出可填入相应空白处的最佳选项。

(一)

Information is crucial(关键的) to the performance(业绩) of supply chain because it provides the facts that supply chain managers use to make decisions. Without information, the managers will not know what customers want, how much inventory is in stock, and when more products will be produced and shipped. In short, without information, the managers can only make decisions blindly. Therefore information makes the supply chain visible(明显的) to the managers.

Given this visibility(鉴于这种可见性), the managers can make decisions to improve the supply chain's performance. Without information, it is impossible for a supply chain to deliver products effectively to customers. With information, companies have the visibility to make decisions to improve overall(全面的) performance of supply chain. In this sense, information is the most important drivers of the supply chain, no other drivers can achieve a higher level of performance.

根据短文内容选择问题最合适的答语。

(　　)1) Tom: Is information crucial(关键的) to the performance of supply chain?
　　　　Jane: _____.
　　　　A. Yes   B. No
　　　　C. Not mentioned   D. No, I don't think so

(　　)2) Tom: Who will not know what customers want without information?
　　　　Jane: _____.
　　　　A. A purchase   B. A manager
　　　　C. A clerk   D. A keeper

(　　)3) Tom: A manager can make decisions to _____ the supply chain's performance, given this visibility.
　　　　A. reduce   B. minimize   C. improve   D. lower

(　　)4) Tom: Is it impossible for a supply chain to deliver products effectively to customers without information?
　　　　Jane: _____.
　　　　A. No mentioned   B. I don't think so
　　　　C. No   D. Yes

(　　)5) Tom: What can achieve a high level of performance?
　　　　Jane: _____.
　　　　A. Information   B. Driver   C. 3PL   D. Purchasing

(二)

A: Hello. Welcome to Wuxi.
B: Can I speak to Tom?
A: Speaking.
B: This is Liyuan Electronics Co. of Xinyang.
A: Have you received the request from the Guangzhou Customs House(海关) regarding(关于)the survey of your cargo?
B: Yes. But is it a condition to go through the custom clearance procedures?

A：Yes, of course. The Customs House must make sure that the goods you sent to be exported conform to(符合)what is stated（规定）on the airway bill.

B：But the consignment(托付货物) is very small, only 90 kilograms of CDs.

A：It is the rule that each and every consignment for export shall be inspected（检查）before leaving China.

B：Can't you put in a word for us? You are our freight forwarder(货运代理人) for so many years and…

A：Sorry. But that is not the rules of the game. You had better send someone here as soon as possible. Otherwise, you'll risk incurring warehousing expense.

B：OK，Wang Huigang from our export department will be with you this afternoon.

A：I will be in my office then. Bye-bye.

B：Bye-bye.

阅读对话回答下列问题：

( )6) — How much do CDs weigh（重）?
 — _____.
   A. 90 kilograms   B. 10 kilograms   C. 1000 grams   D. 100 grams

( )7) — Does Tom's cargo conform to(符合)what is stated（规定）on the airway bill?
 — _____.
   A. Yes   B. Not mentioned   C. Too heavy   D. Too old

( )8) — When will each and every consignment for export be inspected?
 — _____.
   A. After leaving custom house   B. Before leaving the factory
   C. Before leaving China   D. After leaving China

( )9) — Who will be with Tom this afternoon?
 — _____.
   A. A manager   B. A keeper
   C. An agent   D. Wang Huigang

( )10) — Can Tom help Liyuan from Electronics Co. of Xinyang?
 — _____.
   A. Yes   B. No
   C. Of course can D. Not mentioned

三、物流术语英汉翻译(共10小题,每题2分,共20分)

1. the standard unit _____
2. insurance policy _____
3. real time tracing _____
4. Bar Code _____
5. Electronic Order System _____
6. core business _____

7. 税率 _____
8. 信息流 _____
9. 提单 _____
10. 分销商 _____

四、匹配题(共 5 小题,每题为 2 分,共 10 分)

从第 Ⅱ 栏里找到与第一栏一致的翻译

Ⅰ	Ⅱ
1. FCL	A. 门到门服务
2. packing list	B. 贸易协定
3. door to door service	C. 整箱服务
4. trade agreement	D. 断货
5. out of stock	E. 装箱单

1—(   ) 2—(   ) 3—(   ) 4—(   ) 5—(   )

五、回答问题(共 5 小题,每题为 2 分,共 10 分)

1. — Can using container reduce manpower?
   — _____

2. — What is "bill of lading" for short(简写)?
   — _____

3. — What types do global intermediaries include?
   — _____

4. — What refers to the applications of modern information technology in each logistics operation?
   — _____

5. — Is information important in logistics?
   — _____

六、英汉翻译题(共 5 小题,每题为 2 分,共 10 分)

1. Our offer is CIF American main ports.
_____

2. Bill of lading is a document of title for the goods.
_____

3. Shipping agents facilitate the movement of goods through customs.
_____

4. 世界上几乎每个公司在某种程度都要涉及国际贸易。(be involved, to some extent)
_____

5. 请联系船运公司确保装运时间。
_____

附录G 答案 Appendix G

Unit One

1. Translate the following phrases/sentences into Chinese/English.

1) 流通加工价值　　2) Production Logistics　　3) 装卸

4) Supply Logistics　　5) 第三利润源　　6) information processing

7) Logistics is so important that no marketing or production can succeed without logistics support.

8) 我认为现代物流在世界上是最富有挑战性和最激动人心的工作之一。

9) 物流就是为了花最小的成本,把恰当的货物、在恰当的时间、以恰当的方式高效率地进行递送或保存到恰当的地方。

10) The modern logistics plays an important role on the stage of global economy.

2. Answer the following questions in English.

1) In Logistics terms, logistics means the physical movement of goods from the supplier point to the receiver point.

2) Supply Logistics, Production Logistics, Distribution Logistics, Returned Logistics and Waste Material Logistics.

3) No.

4) It includes transportation, storage, distribution, loading and unloading, packaging, information processing, etc.

3. Choose the best answers.

1) D　2) C　3) B　4) B　5) D　6) D　7) B　8) A　9) D　10) A

4. Reading Passage.

1) A　2) C　3) A

Unit Two

1. Translate the following phrases/sentences into Chinese/English.

1) 工业包装　　2) integrated logistics　　3) 销售包装(商业包装)

4) logistics decision　　5) 服务质量,服务水平　　6) package material

7) 包装就是用较低的成本和合理的手段以确保货物在途安全,最终能够把完好无损的货物递交消费者的一种措施。

8) There are two forms of packaging: industrial packaging and consumer packaging.

9) 包装的尺寸、形状和材料都会对工人的作业效率有较大的影响。

10) Consumer packaging assists in marketing, promoting the product, advertising and giving information to customers.

2. Answer the following questions in English.

1) In short, packaging is "a mean of ensuring safe delivery of a product to the consumer in sound condition and at minimum cost".

2) Finding his goods damaged or part missing could make buyer upset most.

3) It is a complimentary (uncritical) role.

4) Because production employees often package the goods.

3. Choose the best answers according to description.

1) C   2) B   3) D   4) C   5) C   6) D   7) D   8) B   9) D   10) D

4. Reading Passage.

1) C   2) B   3) C

Unit Three

1. Translate the following phrases/sentences into Chinese/English.

1) 货架   2) 私有仓库   3) 入库操作   4) deliver-center warehouse

5) return on investment   6) inventory management   7) 将来我想当仓库管理员。

8) 人是仓储的最重要的组成部分。

9) I would like to visit a warehouse with teachers.

10) Warehouse is very important for a firm.

2. Answer the following questions in English.

1) A warehouse keeper.   2) Modern.   3) Yes.   4) Three.

3. Choose the best answers according to description.

1) B   2) D   3) C   4) B   5) A   6) B   7) D   8) A   9) A   10) C

4. Reading Passage.

1) A   2) B   3) D

Unit Four

1. Translate the following phrases/sentences into Chinese/English.

1) 订单处理   2) 储存型配送中心   3) 增值服务

4) data in real time   5) order picking   6) express distribution

7) 废物运输机是配送中心的设备之一。

8) 现在你能与我们订销售协议吗?

9) Let's go to visit a distribution center!

10) Don't worry about the credit of the buyers.

2. Answer the following questions in English.

1) In detail, it is a large and automated center destined to receive goods from various plants and suppliers, take orders, fulfil orders efficiently, and deliver goods to customers on time.

2) Its main function is to carry on physical distribution.

3) Operation flow of distribution has stock, loading, unloading and handling, storage, order procession, picking, replenishment, distribution processing, diseribution and delivery.

4) We used to buy your food products through the export corporations.

3. Choose the best answers according to description.

1) C 2) A 3) B 4) D 5) C 6) B 7) A 8) C 9) D 10) B

4. Reading Passage.

1) C 2) D 3) B

Unit Five

1. Translate the following phrases/sentences into Chinese/English.

1) transportation   2) logistics activity   3) 运输方式

4) 消费地点   5) 顾客,消费者   6) logistician

7) 廉价高效的运输所带来的广阔市场导致生产成本降低。

8) Transportation usually represents the most important single element in logistics activity for most firms.

9) 如果一个产品不移到消费地,那么这个产品对于潜在的客户就没有多大价值。

10) There are five transportation modes—motor, rail, air, water, and pipeline.

2. Answer the following questions in English.

1) It is a critical role.

2) Considering and understanding the matters of transportation.

3) Changing the position of goods and making it available when the customers need them.

4) Accelerating migration of the population and improving efficiency of production.

3. Choose the best answers according to description.

1) A 2) A 3) D 4) B 5) B 6) B 7) A 8) A 9) A 10) C

4. Reading Passage.

1) C 2) D 3) A

Unit Six

1. Translate the following phrases/sentences into Chinese/English.

1) 国际物流   2) 卸货港   3) 实行更优良的配送

4) book the shipping space   5) CIF   6) the standard unit

7) 当今,许多企业不得不加入国际市场。

8) 随着国际贸易的扩大,我们与第三方物流合作非常频繁。

9) We need to find an international freight forwarder.

10) In the transportation of international trade, people load goods with the containers.

2. Answer the following questions in English.

1) An agent.　　2) The port of unloading.　　3) I think it is heavy.　　4) Four.

3. Choose the best answers according to description.

1) B　2) C　3) C　4) D　5) D　6) B　7) A　8) C　9) A　10) B

4. Reading Passage.

1) C　2) B　3) A

Unit Seven

1. Translate the following phrases/sentences into Chinese/English.

1) 常用结尾客套语　　2) 货物的物权凭证　　3) 转运提单

4) shipper　　5) consignee　　6) consignor

7) 谢谢给我这么多详细的解释。

8) 提单是来自承运人(对货物)已装船的收据。

9) Insurance policy is important for the buyers.

10) I have learned so much about documents.

2. Answer the following questions in English.

1) It means "直达提单".　　2) Three.

3) It is to give an inventory of the shipped goods and is required by the customs.

4) Yes, it is.

3. Choose the best answers according to description.

1) A　2) B　3) C　4) D　5) C　6) A　7) B　8) C　9) D　10) D

4. Reading Passage.

1) B　2) A　3) C

Unit Eight

1. Translate the following phrases/sentences into Chinese/English.

1) information technology　　2) Transportation Management System (TMS)

3) data base　　4) 条形码　　5) 控制技术　　6) 信息处理

7) 战术层信息主要用来辅助企业中层管理者制定中短期计划,如预测、生产计划和资源计划。

8) 在信息技术的帮助下前置时间降低。

9) In daily life, information technology helps improve the quality of our life greatly.

10) The development of information technology really makes us feel more efficient, more convenient and safer.

2. Answer the following questions in English.

1) Yes.

2) It includes Bar Code, Radio Frequency Identification technology, Global Positioning System, Geographic Information System.

3) It must be accurate, accessible, timely and of the right kind.

4) Seven.

3. Choose the best answers according to description.

1) D   2) C   3) D   4) D   5) C   6) C   7) D   8) C   9) B   10) C

4. Reading passage.

1) D   2) B   3) D

期中试题答案

一、单项选择

1. B   2. B   3. B   4. C   5. D   6. D   7. A   8. A   9. D   10. D

二、阅读理解

1. D   2. C   3. D   4. D   5. D   6. A   7. B   8. C   9. D   10. A

三、物流术语英汉翻译

1. 增值服务   2. 物流系统   3. 客户服务   4. 消费包装   5. 成品

6. warehousing   7. distribution center   8. protect goods

9. inventory management   10. logistics decision

四、匹配题

1. D   2. E   3. A   4. C   5. B

五、回答问题

1. Yes, it can.   2. Yes, it does.   3. Logistics does.

4. Receiving, transfer, storage, picking and shipping.   5. 7 steps.

六、英汉翻译题

1. 物流是独特的全球通道。

2. 消费包装指的也是内部包装或销售包装。

3. 我们能为你提供多种多样的货物库存。

4. Distribution centers perform a great number of value-added activities.

5. Logistics management will evolve to the global supply chain.

期末试题答案

一、单项选择

1. A   2. B   3. C   4. D   5. D   6. C   7. A   8. D   9. B   10. B

二、阅读理解

1. A   2. B   3. C   4. D   5. A   6. A   7. B   8. C   9. D   10. B

三、物流术语英汉翻译

1. 标箱   2. 保险单   3. 实时跟踪   4. 条形码   5. 电子自动订货系统

6. 核心业务   7. duty rates   8. information flow   9. bill of lading

10. distributor

四、匹配题

1. C   2. E   3. A   4. B   5. D

五、回答问题

1. Yes, it can.   2. It is B/L.

3. International freight forwarders, export management companies, customs brokers and shipping agents.

4. LIT.   5. Yes, it is.

六、英汉翻译题

1. 我们的报价是美国主要港口到岸价。

2. 提单是物权凭证。

3. 船运代理人帮助顾客完成货物通过海关的各种手续。

4. Almost every company in the world is involved in international trade to some extent.

5. Please contact the shipping company to confirm the shipment time.

参考文献

[1] 唐四元.现代物流技术与装备[M].北京:清华大学出版社,2010.
[2] 陈志群.物流与配送[M].北京:高等教育出版社,2008.
[3] 刘莉.仓储管理实务[M].北京:中国物资出版社,2009.
[4] 牛红星.物流员、助理物流师职业技能鉴定考试指南[M].广东:新世纪出版社,2009.
[5] 闫静雅.物流专业英语[M].北京:机械工业出版社,2010.
[6] 牛国崎.物流专业英语[M]. 北京:北京理工大学出版社,2009.
[7] 高本河,缪立新,卢锦石.物流专业英语与计算机基础[M]. 深圳:海天出版社,2006.
[8] 程世平.物流专业英语[M]. 北京:机械工业出版社,2003.
[9] 卢楠.现代物流基础[M]. 北京:北京邮电大学出版社,2008.
[10] 吴健.现代物流专业英语[M]. 北京:机械工业出版社,2009.